Walk!

Mallorca West

with

Charles Davis

DISCOVERY WALKING GUIDES LTD

Walk! Mallorca West
First Edition - January 2005

Copyright © 2005 Charles Davis

Published by
Discovery Walking Guides Ltd
10 Tennyson Close, Northampton NN5 7HJ,
England

Maps
Copyright © 2005 David & Ros Brawn

Photographs
Photographs in this book were taken by the author,
Charles Davis, and Jeanette Tallegas.

Front Cover Photographs

Port de Banyalbufar
(Walk 25)

Tour of Puig Gros d'en
Bendinat (Walk 3)

Camí de Graner del Delme
(Walk 5c)

Broom, lavender and
gladioli on Cap
Andritxol(Walk 9)

ISBN 1-899554-98-X

Text and photographs* © Charles Davis 2005

Maps © David & Ros Brawn

Walk! Mallorca West

CONTENTS

THE WALKS

CALVIÀ AND THE SOUTHERN COAST

Charles Davis was born in London, and has lived and worked in the United States, Sudan, Turkey, Ivory Coast, Spain and France. With the onset of middle age, he realised that the urge to roam was better satisfied by walking than bouncing about on the back of a lorry in the middle of the desert, and now divides his time between mountain tops, desk-tops and laptops. He is the author of numerous highly praised and wholly unpublished novels.

Jeanette Tallegas has spent thirty odd years labouring for the French education system, from which she has finally, gleefully, taken early retirement. Asked what she intends doing now, she resolutely replies, "Nothing". Nonetheless, she does follow the author up various gruelling mountains, frequently alarming younger ramblers who seem to assume that remote and inaccessible places are the preserve of youth.

Charles Davis is also the author of:

34 Alpujarras Walks

Walk! La Gomera

and

Walk! Mallorca (North & Mountains)

published by Discovery Walking Guides

One shouldn't necessarily trust numbers, still less celebrity, yet when such disparate figures as George Sand, Frederic Chopin, Ruben Darí Miguel de Unamuno, Robert Graves, Ava Gardner, Freya Stark, King Juan Carlos, John Noakes, Peter Stringfellow, Richard Branson, Andrew Lloyd-Webber, Michael Douglas, Claudia Schiffer, Ralph Schumacher, Caroline Corr and Bob Geldof, choose to spend anything from a prolonged season to a lifetime in a given place, there must be something going on that's worth investigating. A more mismatched assembly of fame would be hard to imagine, yet all have found a temporary or permanent retreat in Mallorca. And this the island that was at the same time a byword for mass tourism. There are, of course, other places popular with both celebrities and crowds, but Mallorca is distinguished by a remarkable capacity for absorbing outside influence without losing its distinctive personality, a capacity that has as much to do with the ingenuity and adaptability of its people as the gifts bestowed on the island by nature.

The Balearic Islands get their name from the Greek word for slingshot, a weapon the original inhabitants employed to such deadly effect they were permanently identified with it and earned a place alongside the elephants in Hannibal's army. They owed their facility to a custom whereby the food of young *Balears* was placed in the uppermost branches of tall trees. If they couldn't knock it down with a slingshot, they did without. This uncompromising training produced an ingenious people who understood that if you didn't adapt to circumstances, you went hungry. It's a message that has been passed down through the generations, shaping not just the island's economy and the character of its people but the very landscape itself.

On Mallorca, mountains that would elsewhere have been dismissed as a wilderness best left to misfits, hermits and bandits, were embraced as a refuge from invading armies and marauding pirates, whose arrival was heralded from the watchtowers that still punctuate the coastline. On Mallorca, a topography any sane plains-dwelling farmer would tell you is too precipitous to be cultivated, was portioned out, scored with terraces, enclosed by some of the most improbably perpendicular walls you will ever see, and turned into valuable farmland. On Mallorca, tiny niches in otherwise impenetrable cliffs, were dubbed with indomitable optimism 'ports' and transformed into focal points for fishing, communication and trade. On Mallorca, even the most inhospitable terrain was home to hundreds of families scraping (often as not literally) a living from the land, their painstaking labour progressively tracing out the charcoal-burners' and lime-firers' tracks, transhumance trails, pilgrims ways and neighbourly paths that are now one of the island's most vital resources. And if a covey of international engineering experts declared a spring could not be canalized, it was inevitably only a matter of time before a Mallorcan pig farmer proved them wrong. The genius and obstinacy of this people are invincible. All you have to do is say *can't* and they set about finding a way one *can*.

When agriculture went into decline and poverty loomed, Mallorcans concluded that if one could no longer export the fruits of sunshine to wealthy foreigners, one must import wealthy foreigners to the fruits of sunshine. At a time when the inhabitants of Torremolinos and Tossa del Mar were still mending their nets and reckoning the cost of another pair of rope-soled sandals, Mallorcans came up with the bright idea that one could sell such intangible and apparently unpackageable assets as light and heat, and set about inventing mass tourism. And then, when environmental radicalism was promoted to orthodoxy and everybody agreed that mass tourism wasn't necessarily an unparalleled Good Thing, it was Mallorca that pioneered the shift upmarket to quality holidays and eco-friendly tourism, reinventing itself as Europe's most popular warm island walking destination. If that's not adaptability, I don't know what is.

Most walkers head for the rugged northern coast and central **Tramuntana** detailed in our Walk! Mallorca (North & Mountains) Guidebook, but there is another walking area in the west of the island where the **Tramuntana** peters out in wooded slopes framing tightly clustered villages linked by dozens of tracks, trails and paths. Apart from one or two classic itineraries such as **Galatzó** and **Sa Trapa**, this bucolic landscape is less famous among ramblers, but though the terrain is less dramatic, the walking is equally gratifying, appealing to a gentler, more contemplative mindset. This is not the place to come if you want to test yourself or have a compelling urge to get-to-the-top, though you will break out in a sweat once in a while and there are several itineraries that should satisfy even the most gung-ho rambler; nor is it an area generally characterized by the savage grandeur encountered further east, though you will find your breath-taken by more than mere exertion; but if you're after tranquility, if your tastes tend toward the domestic and rural, if the silhouette of a tall green pine set against an infinite expanse of blue is likely to set your mind at rest, if you like little coves tucked between impressive cliffs, if the mazy jigsaw of a sun-dappled forest floor is balm to your eyes, if tidy terraced valleys and picturesque hamlets please you, then Western Mallorca could have been made for you.

WHEN TO GO

Given the fierce heat of summer, September to May is the ramblers' season. Autumn and spring are best for birdwatching, April and May for lovers of wild flowers. Winters are generally mild and dry.

GETTING THERE, GETTING ABOUT, GETTING A BED

Charter, charter, charter: only for a very long stay will it be worth bringing your own car rather than renting, since the ferries from Barcelona and Sè are costly - and with 80,000 hire cars available on the island, you should be able to find something to suit your budget. The bus service is excellent in this area and nearly all itineraries can be reached by public transport (Walks 1, 2 & 22b require private transport, Walks 11, 21, 22a, & 30 involve additional road-walking if arriving by bus), though extracting a comprehensive timetable from the information desk in **Palma** bus station requires the inquisitorial skills of a Torquemada. Accommodation is plentiful and easily organized privately, on-line, over the phone or on the spot. Get the picture? Torquemada notwithstanding, everything's easy here and if you want a cheap, hassle free walking holiday with no major logistical problems, look no further.

We've aimed to provide a good spread of walks covering three key areas within the region and there should be sufficient walks within each area to fill an average holiday. However, given the region's relatively small size and good bus service, no area is exclusive of another and I recommend moving about to get a taste of the varying landscapes. The walks are equally varied, ranging from short strolls suitable for walkers of all ages and aptitudes, to rough high-mountain itineraries only recommended for experienced ramblers.

Timings are all 'pure' timings excluding snacking, snapping and simply standing still staring. It is highly unlikely you will complete any of these walks in exactly the time specified. Before you tackle the longer routes, time yourself against one of our shorter itineraries, then curse me for a slowcoach or a racing maniac as seems appropriate. All global timings include the return unless otherwise specified.

The paths are generally well-maintained and clearly signposted, though waymarking is frequently faint and sparing. Painted waymarks tend to have been done by German rambling groups while stone cairns are the preferred method of Mallorcan ramblers. The latter are more natural, more frequent and often more reliable, though there is a tendency for enthusiasts to leave cairns wherever they happened to have walked, no matter how alarming the landscape. Each local authority has its own system of marking routes, ranging from rather rickety hand-painted mapboards to sturdy GR-style wooden posts. Since my routes do not necessarily correspond to the traditional walk, only follow waymarks when they are referred to in the text.

The GR-212 or 'Way of the Dry Stones', which runs the length of the island, follows the mountains behind the northern coast from **Port d'Andratx** to **Valldemossa**. It's reasonably well wayposted, but is not specifically waymarked and is occasionally disputed. The wayposts have been painted red-and-yellow rather than the customary red-and-white. The route is not yet complete and since negotiations concerning rights of way were still pending at the time of publication we were unable to include the **Esporles** to **Valldemossa** walk as we had intended. There is also a long stretch on the road between the **Coll de sa Gramola** and **Estellencs**. There are various plans to remedy this, but none have as yet been realized.

Part of the fun of walking in Mallorca is spotting itineraries as you drive around and, though nearly all the key routes in the region are covered in the present publication, you should keep your eyes peeled for walks I haven't described, either because they were too short to merit a discrete itinerary number, or because they are disputed (but still practicable for enterprising individuals!), or (hopefully) because they are new routes opened up after our researches were completed.

The descriptions are fairly detailed, largely because this area is densely populated and human impact means more junctions and crossroads. I've tried to give enough detail for those who need confirmation they're on the right path, but not so much as to irritate more confidant pathfinders with superfluity. For ease of reference, street names at the start of walks and place names are shown as bold text, while place names seen on signs are enclosed in single quotes. *Italics* are used for *discrete Spanish words*, which if also shown in *purple*, are explained in the glossary. Consistency rather than deficient vocabulary accounts for all climbs being 'gentle', 'steady', or 'steep'.

EQUIPMENT

No special equipment is required for these walks, but see Discovery Walking Guides' recommendations on Page 26.

PROBLEMS

Violent crime is rare, but petty theft is epidemic. Never leave valuables in your car.

Access to private land can be a problem. As a general rule, we have excluded all walks where access is restricted or potentially controversial. Like most rules, this one is proved-by-the-exception, honoured-in-the-breach, and generally ignored when convenient. 'Convenience' does not mean I was short of itineraries and needed to pad the book out regardless of a walk's practicality. It does mean that, in two instances, I decided to include walks where a right of way has been disputed but has remained open due to legal action or sheer force of numbers. In both cases, an uncontroversial option is cited. If, despite our best efforts, we have chosen a route subsequently closed off, please let us know.

FLORA & FAUNA

Carritx is the pampas-like grass (*Ampelodesmus mauritanica*) found all over the island. The classic trick with *carritx* is to stand on it with one foot and trip over it with the other. Otherwise, the most common or distinctive flowers, shrubs and herbs are asphodels, euphorbia (or spurge), mastic tree (*Pistacia lentisus*), gladioli, wild garlic, lavender, myrtle, thyme, rosemary, foxglove, rocket, vetch, St. John's Wort, sarsaparilla *(Smilax aspera),* hellebore, windflowers and blue tobacco. There are enough orchids to merit a book to themselves. The pyramidal orchid *Anacamtis pyramidalis* is most common, the purple giant orchid can be seen on the slopes of **Galatzó** and one is supposed to be able to see bee orchids and tongue orchids. In April the island is awash with brilliant flowering mimosa, jacaranda and Judas trees, but on the whole, the most common trees in the mountains are pine, holm oak, strawberry trees, almond, oleaster and olive. Perhaps the most common vegetation is mixed scrub. Specialist publications differentiate between 'wild olive & Cneorum' scrub and 'rosemary & heather' scrub, but the distinction was too fine for my eye, most scrub being composed of *carritx*, mastic trees and cistus, and in rockier more exposed areas, asphodels.

Mallorca is justly famous as a bird watcher's paradise, however most of the key locations for 'twitchers' are in the high mountains and the north-east. In our area, you will see warblers, shearwater, thrushes, swallows, martins, partridge, several varieties of sparrow, abundant finches and tits, and possibly the wonderfully endearing hoopoe, with his comical crest and dipping, gravity challenged flight that always seems to be just one flap of the wings away from disaster. The most common birds of prey seen in this area are kites, kestrels, peregrine falcons, and (on **Dragonera**), Eleanora's falcons. You may also see bearded, griffon and Egyptian vultures, booted eagles and osprey.

As for mammals, reptiles and amphibians, despite proud boasts about genet and pine marten, the chances are the only thing you'll see in this line are feral cats - that is domestic cats run wild rather than true feral cats. Considering they're regarded as a pest and don't get many genteel old ladies leaving them saucers' of milk, they look surprising healthy. Farmers used to poison them (and, of course, anything else that took the bait), but the authorities have an enlightened attitude to controlling the population, capturing and neutering the cats, giving the kittens away and releasing the adults back into the wild. In previous visits we have also seen weasels and shrews.

From the tops of the mountains to twenty metres from the more remote coastline, you will see (and in spring when they're rutting hear) plenty of wild or semi-wild goats and, on some of the more remote mountain tops, sheep that seem to have run wild, too.

On **Cap de Cala Figuera** (Walk 4) we saw a spur-thighed tortoise ambling about as if he owned the place, which I rather hope he did. Signs suggest tortoises can be seen elsewhere, but then signs suggest all sorts of things that don't necessarily bear much relation to reality.

We heard plenty of frogs and toads, but only saw one and that in the wholly improbable location of **Pujol des Gat** (se Walk 1).

Snakes are rare and not dangerous.

Sightings of whales and dolphins are occasionally reported.

EATING & DRINKING

It would be entirely possible to spend a full year on Mallorca without eating anything more alien than bacon and eggs, but assuming you fancy something more adventurous, the following notes might help get you started.

Sopa (soup) *mallorquin* is pretty much a vegetable stew and a good filling meal in itself, while *sopa de matances* and *sopa de pescado* are respectively the meat and fish equivalents. *Allioli* is garlic mayonnaise and *fonoi marí* is pickled sea fennel. *Pa amb oli* is dear to the Mallorca sense of self, but is not that exceptional, just the usual bread and oil found everywhere else in Spain: 'just', I say – it's very good, especially with *charcuterie* or a few slices of *Mahón*, a salty hard cheese. *Arroz Brut* is the local paella, *tumbat* is a variation on the classic Mediterranean combination of aubergine and tomatoes, and *greixonera* is a casserole. Beef (*ternera*) is a waste of time, but pork (*cerdo* or *porc*) and lamb (*cordero* or *anyell*) are excellent. *Butifarra* or *morcilla* is black-pudding and *sobrasada,* a local specialty, is a kind of *chorizo*-sausage pâé Where Mallorcans really excel though is at the baker's: *ensaïmadas* are light breakfast pastries, often copied elsewhere in Spain, but rarely done as well. *Coca* is the local crumbly-based, vegetable-topped version of pizza (the green topping is a mixture of shard, leek and lashings of parsley) and makes an excellent picnic snack, as do the vegetable pasties (*cocarrois*), and meat and fish pies (*empanada*).

Given the island's popularity with Germans, there is plenty of good foreign beer available. Of the local varieties, the well-known San Miguel is a bit soapy and not nearly as good as Estrella, brewed by the Barcelona based Damm, who also produce the more potent Voll-Damm. Mallorcan wine can be excellent, notably those from the **Binissalem** denomination, our favourites being the *Autentico* and *Vino Veritas* of Jose L. Ferrer. *Es Có* from **Valldemossa** is good, too. *Hierbas* is the local digestive, a herb flavoured anisette.

TOURIST STUFF

There are dozens of general books about Mallorca, but if you don't care to carry a small library round with you, the following suggestions might help fill in a day off. The old town of **Palma** is definitely worth wandering around for an afternoon and almost obligatory is a visit to the splendid cathedral, restored by Gaudi with such good taste even the architecturally illiterate contemplate it with reverence. Equal weight should be given to some of the villages, notably **Estellencs** and **Banyalbufar** on the northern coast, which both reward a little time spent ferreting around. Given that this book skirts the heartland of Mallorcan mass-tourism, the conventional diversions are legion, notably on the southern coast, where there are enough water-parks, golf courses, themed bars, and shops selling sandals, straw hats, lewd 'novelties' and cheap booze to satisfy the shopaholics, leisure fiends and inebriates of an entire continent, let alone a small Mediterranean island. Glass-bottomed boats ply their trade from most of the large ports, while those who wish to see how more elevated life forms spend their time might like to visit **La Reserva** country park near **Puigpunyent** and the **Sa Granja** manor house near **Esporles**. Mallorca is famous for its leather goods, but of particular interest to the rambler will be the Bestard factory in **Lloseta**, where they make what are commonly acknowledged to be the best walking boots available in Spain.

LANGUAGE

English is spoken in most bars, restaurants and shops, but once you're out in the countryside, it's Spanish, Catalán or pantomime. Everywhere, a few words of Spanish will take you a long way, and a few Catalán phrases even further. Mallorcan Catalán is a less harsh version of the mainland variety, as is the linguistic politics of the islanders, who are not disgruntled if they have to speak Spanish.

ACKNOWLEDGEMENTS

My thanks to Jeannette for creating a home in circumstances that were limited, itinerant and probably prohibited, to Ros and David for their usual steady support, and to the countless Mallorcan ramblers and lovers of nature, without whom this island would long since have been covered in concrete apart from a few heavily fenced reserves dedicated to the preservation of the super-rich.

CALVIÀ AND THE SOUTHERN COAST

A rapid clockwise tour round our region beginning in **Palma** is a bit like a review of man's relationship with the natural world over the last several hundred years. The easily accessible coast between **Palma** and **Port d'Andratx** is so very accessible that it was chosen as the site for Mallorca's experiment in mass tourism, and resembles a museum recording the late twentieth century's evolving notions of appropriate leisure facilities, ranging from water-parks, sun-loungers and duty-free shops to golf courses, walking trails and cycle routes. Further west lies a less domestic landscape that has, to some extent, been shaped by generations of gruelling labour, but remains sufficiently impenetrable to have resisted the new kid on the block, King Concrete, and which has been a celebrated walking area for nearly a century, since rambling first developed in Spain as an expression of regional identity. And beyond that, in the north, the topography is so wild and set about by high mountains and steep cliffs, that man has simply had to accommodate himself to the available space, now as in the past, fitting in as best he can and accepting the compromises dictated by an environment that maybe used, even abused, but can only ever be partially tamed. This is a small corner of a small island, but within it we have three distinct regions, each with its own discrete character and history.

The **Calvià** area is often skipped by ramblers heading for more famous walks in the west, which is a pity as it boasts over 100 kilometres of paths, and has a progressive policy of signposting and publicizing selected itineraries - in one case, the *ayuntamiento* even pays landowners to let tourists cross their estates (see Appendix E). A cursory glance would suggest the coast has been surrendered to property developers with badly ruptured imaginations, yet tucked behind what can at times seem a rather drab facade are some lovely little creeks and several wooded headlands that offer a surprising number of very pleasant short walks. And the more you explore, the more unspoiled corners you encounter.

What's more, the *costa* living (excuse the pun) has not been as dear as one might have feared. Apart from one lamentable exception that lives up to everything it aspires to be, most of the package resorts have, with typical Mallorcan dexterity, made enough money to escape the worst consequences of their history, reinvesting in the sort of infrastructure and services that would only be found in other sunspots once they had become the preserve of the super-rich.

Meanwhile, one only has to head a kilometre or so inland to forget you are anywhere near a tourist resort and to enjoy a largely bucolic landscape of quiet country lanes, rolling hills and small but dramatic mountains (see Walks 5, 6, 8 & 10). The town of **Calvià** itself is a pleasant, strangely subdued place, and worth strolling around, notably to admire the distinctive twin towers of the local church. As for the neighbouring village of **Capdella**, that has been so tastefully and respectfully occupied by second-home owners, only an unusually high proportion of blue eyes and blonde hair suggests it is anything other than a traditional Spanish village.

In rambling terms, this is one of those areas that has never been quite spectacular enough to lure the large hiking parties, leaving its hidden charms to the appreciation of local residents and those in the know. One of the most neglected areas is the **Na Burguesa** ridge, right on the doorstep of **Palma**, which despite a succession of devastating fires remains a superb hiking area, particularly suited to mid-winter walking (see Walks 1-3). The other key hiking areas are **Cap de Cal Figuera** (Walks 4&7) and **Cap Andritxol**, the first a one-time military zone now largely open to the public, the second the site of a much publicized tussle between money and a man with a pair of wire-cutters (see Walk 9).

In general, walks in this area are through a classic Mediterranean landscape of low ridges and rocky coastline thinly covered with pine. Wild it ain't (though we did see a spur-thighed tortoise strolling about with an insouciance that suggested the pet industry had never existed), but if one takes a moment to look just that little bit further round the corner, there's enough untenanted land to satisfy all but the most Eden-seeking of ramblers, and a good ten-day walking holiday could be pieced together from itineraries in this region alone.

ANDRATX AND THE (WILDISH) WEST

Andratx enjoys a better reputation among ramblers than **Calvià**, though it must be said that some of the damage done to the coastline here is as reckless as you'll find anywhere. The **Urbanización Gran Folies** smeared over the hillside above **Cala d'es Llamp** can only really be commended for the refreshing honesty of its name, while the attractive, well-maintained resort of **Camp de Mar** is almost (but not quite) overwhelmed by the disproportionately large hotel looming over its diminutive beach. On the whole though, this is an area that deserves its reputation as a tranquil bolt hole to be contrasted with the busier resorts on which the island first built its reputation.

Port d'Andratx (Walks 10 & 11), until comparatively recently a small unspoiled fishing harbour, now pulls off the difficult trick of being a sunny suburb for both Bonn and London, where wealthy foreigners moor their power-cruisers and swan about endeavouring to conjure the chic ambience of St. Tropez in the sixties. The atmosphere won't be to everybody's taste, but it remains a picturesque and generally peaceful spot.

A little further north lies **Sant Elm** (Walk 12), which is even more diminutive and still (just) identifiable as a fishing hamlet. Inevitably, the 'fishing hamlet' is now flanked by villas and flats, and is sprouting cranes like asphodels, but development does seem to be controlled and the abandoned *urbanización* to the north (Walk 16) has become a favourite with local people walking their dogs, so riddling it with paths it resembles a blueprint for a respectable maze. Even if you don't do a walk here, it's worth spending an afternoon or evening strolling along the coast, watching the fishing smacks returning home, trailing their confetti of seagulls, or enjoying the sunset over the splendid little island of **Dragonera**.

Rising out of the sea like the ragged fin of a dyspeptic sea-monster that's swallowed one shipful of mariners too many, **Dragonera** is one of the most spectacular sights in the western Mediterranean. The name is said to have been inspired either by its shape or by the thousands of Balearic lizards that live there, but whatever its etymology, it's a very protean lump of rock, generally resembling a pronounced spine, but from certain angles looking like the nose of a giant stingray surging out of the sea. Don't be put off by the island's rather dry and daunting aspect. It's a lovely place, well administered as a *Parc Natural*, with surprisingly abundant vegetation and a tremendous variety of seabirds. The climb to **Na Pò** (Walk 17), in effect the **Tramuntana**'s first summit and manifestly insurmountable when seen from a distance, is a classic, easy excursion.

Undoubtedly the most celebrated part of this area though is the rugged land behind the **Sa Trapa** monastery (Walks 18-20). Again, a first glance from the road can be discouraging, revealing a few sharp peaks and a lot of fire-scorched terraces, but once you start exploring, you realize quite why this is such a classic rambling area. Composed of complex folds, interleaving summits, dramatic cliffs, sharp escarpments, and peppered with derelict *casetas*, it'the sort of shifting, shapely, living landscape that persuades you every exploration will be rewarded with one more new path, one more hidden corner, one more evocative echo of its agricultural past.

Up the road from **Sant Elm** lies **S'Arraco** (Walks 13, 14 & 19), an attractive, peaceful village with a discreet expatriate population and a faint air of never-never land about it, as if the residents went to bed one night and simply forgot to get up the next day. It's the sort of fairytale fate to which one might easily succumb amid such cozy drowsy countryside, where the terraces have largely been abandoned by farmers without being smothered in villas. Doubtless I'm maligning the locals here, but the most animated residents we saw were a goat and three ducks dozing in the lee of a rundown shed. I'd like to think that's as lively as it gets.

Continuing up the road and crossing the **Coll de s'Arraco** we come to the hub of this area, the small town of **Andratx**, a distinctively Mallorcan locus, slightly sleepy (though not totally somnolent like **S'Arraco**), friendly, and perfectly able to get on with its own life regardless of the tens of thousands of visitors that fall within its administrative orbit. The only real sign that the town is conscious of prestige and standing are two imposing buildings, the old church, reminiscent of a fortified Cathar church, and the new *ayuntamiento* (so imposing it's almost pompous) that stands above the town. Some pleasant strolls can be had along the narrow lanes around **Andratx** (see Walk 10 in the previous section, the start of Walk 20, and Appendix E), while the ridge of the **Garrafa** plateau (Walk 15) has been transformed, thanks to the closure of easier routes to the top, into one of Mallorca's great wild walks.

ESTELLENCS, BANYALBUFAR, ESPORLES & PUIGPUNYENT

This is the wild north, where the **Tramuntana** declares itself in earnest with its first major peaks, **S'Esclop** (Walk 21) and **Galatzó** (Walk 22). The landscape here is more distinctively Mallorcan than in the south, being chiefly composed of high limestone ridges and summits cloaked with dense oak woods riddled with charcoal burners' paths and tracks (see Walks 24, 26, 27,

28 & 30).

Estellencs, the northern gateway to **Galatzó** is an attractive little village clustered round a central knoll surrounded by terraces. Immediately you enter it, you sense it has contrived to develop tourism without denaturing itself. The bars and restaurants are there, but so are the old men staring distractedly at passing tourists as if they are some prodigiously singular and intriguing curiosity. Likewise **Banyalbufar**. Though bigger than **Estellencs** and more replete with tourist-centred services, it's still a village and operates at the leisurely pace its steep streets dictate. It's one of those places where hard practical decisions taken in the past have brought about a picturesque result for the present. Sandwiched between the sea and the mountains, far enough from the coast to be safe from marauding pirates, near enough to maintain contact with the outside world, and situated at the heart of the cultivable land, it's a beautiful village and likely to stay that way since there's little room for building and no room for the infrastructure to support a significantly larger population.

While **Estellencs** and **Banyalbufar** have been touched by tourism thanks to the superb sea views (see Walk 23), the semi-enclaves of **Esporles** and **Puigpunyent** make hardly any concessions at all to a tourist economy and instead simply get on with life as they always have done, inward looking (the mountains make sure there's no outward to look at), self-sufficient, but ready to gather any visitor into the fold if that visitor makes the first step. The only indications that tourists pass through **Estellencs** are the **Sa Granja** manor house, which is open to the public, one very attractive and very stylish *hostal*, and slightly more sophisticated fare than is usual in rural restaurants; as for **Puigpunyent**, as far as I could make out it barely acknowledges the phenomenon at all, apart from the **La Reserva** country park, and is all the better for such unfashionable negligence. These places are bit like the donjon or inner-keep of a castle, to which defenders would retreat when particularly hard-pressed; it's not that the residents are unfriendly, but you get the strong impression that this is the heartland of Mallorca and that the islanders have no intention of contaminating it with the sort of progress that has cluttered up most of the coast.

The extraordinary little road linking these two towns has to be experienced by anyone with wheels. It's so attractive, it even features in a locally produced walking guide as an itinerary! With tiny green fields tucked between dry stone walls and flanked by steep slopes forested with oak, it's the sort of road that makes you wonder whether we weren't better off before we started cutting holes in mountains to make tunnels and motorways, back in the days when you really had to want to go somewhere to get there. Even the property developers, a species not noted for their nostalgia, seem to have realized this, judging by the *urbanización* at **Port d'es Canonge** (Walk 25), the only significant attempt to turn this stretch of the northern coast into a tourist destination. When the American company in charge of it went bankrupt, the project ground to a halt, but you can still see the lines of what was planned and nobody seems to have thought the pace of modern life called for a more direct means of access than the tiny winding lane that already existed. Maybe they were right.

The walks in this area are more energetic and more likely to satisfy the dedicated rambler than the shorter, generally easier itineraries in the south. Extensive use is made of the trails left by lime-firers and charcoal burners, two rural industries that have been crucial in shaping the Mallorcan countryside. Since both industries were based on trees (one ton of lime required up to ten tons of wood) and both were extremely time-consuming (a single firing could last up to two weeks) a whole network of trails was beaten through the great oak woods of the North and the men engaged in this hard and unrewarding work would spend most of their time in the mountains, either actively refining lime or charcoal, or cutting and seasoning the wood they required. The roughly thatched shelters they lived in are now, almost without exception (a restored example is seen on Walk 22), reduced to a mere jumble of stones tumbled against a larger rock, but *sitjes* (charcoal burning circles) and lime-kilns are to be seen everywhere, and though many trails have been lost, many more remain. A visit to Mallorca could not possibly be considered complete without following at least one of these trails (Walks 26 & 27 are particularly recommended): meandering through deep, mazy woodland on a sun-dappled path in a landscape that is at once wild and full of the comforting, ghostly echoes of previous human activity, is an unforgettable experience.

LOCATION MAPS

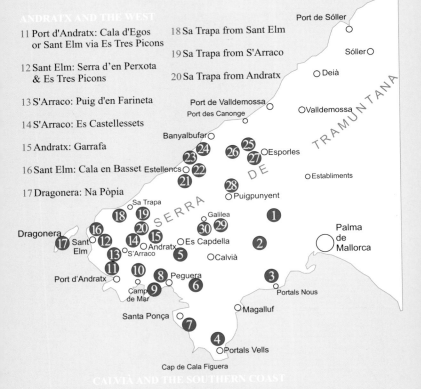

The Balearic Islands

Approximate area
covered by
Walk! Mallorca West

MORE MALLORCA WALKING

For walks in the north and mountains of the island, see Walk! Mallorca North
and Mountains by Charles Davis (ISBN 1-899554-92-0) and Mallorca North
& Mountains Tour & Trail Super-Durable Map (ISBN 1-899554- 93-9), both
published by Discovery Walking Guides Ltd.

MAP NOTES & LEGEND

The map sections used in this book have been designed for this book by Discovery Walking Guides Ltd. For more information on DWG publications, write to DWG Ltd., 10 Tennyson Close, Northampton NN5 7HJ, England, or visit:

www.walking.demon.co.uk   **www.dwgwalking.co.uk**

ALTITUDE, HÖHE, ALTITUD, ALTITUDE

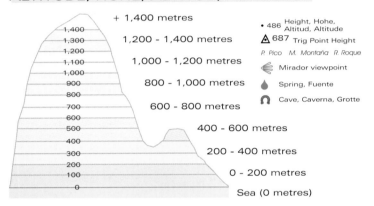

+ 1,400 metres

1,200 - 1,400 metres

1,000 - 1,200 metres

800 - 1,000 metres

600 - 800 metres

400 - 600 metres

200 - 400 metres

0 - 200 metres

Sea (0 metres)

• 486 Height, Hohe, Altitud, Altitude

△ 687 Trig Point Height

P. Pico   M. Montaña   R. Roque

Mirador viewpoint

Spring, Fuente

Cave, Caverna, Grotte

ROADS, STRAßE, CARRETERA, ROUTE

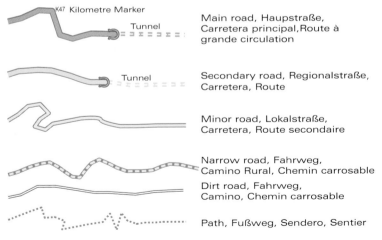

K47 Kilometre Marker

Tunnel

Main road, Haupstraße, Carretera principal, Route à grande circulation

Tunnel

Secondary road, Regionalstraße, Carretera, Route

Minor road, Lokalstraße, Carretera, Route secondaire

Narrow road, Fahrweg, Camino Rural, Chemin carrosable

Dirt road, Fahrweg, Camino, Chemin carrosable

Path, Fußweg, Sendero, Sentier

Walking Routes, Wanderweg, Sendero, Chemin.

Walk! Mallorca West Route (Red) 17

GPS Waypoint
see Waypoint Lists

8

Urban area

Large House, Casa Major — House, Casa — Ruin/Barn/Uninhabited

Lighthouse, Faro — Chapel, Ermita — Church Iglesia — P Parking

Bar/Rest — Hotel — Petrol — Sports Ground, Campo Deportivo

Picnic area, Zona Recreativa — Cemetery, Cementario

Tower, Torre — Camping

our rating for effort/exertion:-
1 very easy   **2** easy   **3** average
4 energetic   **5** strenuous

approximate **time** to complete a walk (compare your times against ours early in a walk) - does not include stopping time

approximate walking **distance** in kilometres

approximate **ascents/descents** in metres (N = negligible)

circular route

linear route (two way unless otherwise marked)

risk of **vertigo**

refreshments (may be at start or end of a route only) (scores between 1-5 for quality of food, service, location or combination of these qualities)

Walk descriptions include:
- timing in minutes, shown as (40M)
- compass directions, shown as (NW)
- heights in metres, shown as (1355m)
- GPS waypoints, shown as (Wp.3)

Notes on the text
Place names are shown in **bold text**, except where we refer to a written sign, when any place names are enclosed in single quotation marks. Spanish words are shown in *italics*, and if also in *purple*, will be included in the glossary at the back of this book.

Mallorca's rolling landscape running into mountains gives the impression that navigation should be easy. On the ground it is a different matter, with high bushes and walls obscuring the view, and a lack of local landmarks to focus on. On some routes we might wish there were fewer paths and choices, rather than the excess with which we are sometimes faced.

While most walking routes are easy to follow with a good route description, some present quite a challenge; **Walk 4, Cap de Cala Figuera**, poses a tough navigational test despite its comparatively flat landscape, while **Walk 9, Peguera: Cap Andritxol** also provides an abundance of navigational choices. Knowing exactly where you are is a great confidence builder when exploring new landscapes. GPS waypoints give you pin-point navigational accuracy, allowing you to enjoy the walking route free from worries about wayfinding.

All The GPS Waypoints quoted in Walk! Mallorca (West) were recorded during the research of the walking routes, and are subject to the general considerations as to the accuracy of GPS units in the location concerned. It is virtually impossible to reproduce the exact GPS Waypoint co-ordinates in practice when walking a route, and 5-10 metres is an acceptable standard of accuracy when you have '3D navigation' (four or more satellites in view) on Mallorca. Only in extreme situations, such as on **Walk 22, Galatzo (a) and (b)** routes, are you likely to experience poor GPS reception and here you can rely upon the detailed walk description.

GPS Waypoint co-ordinates are quoted for the WGS84 datum in degrees and minutes of Latitude and Longitude. To input the Waypoints into your GPS we suggest that you:

- switch on your GPS and select 'simulator' mode, 'demo' mode on some units,

- check that your GPS is set to the WGS84 datum (its default datum) and the ' position format' '° .mm.mmm',

- input the GPS Waypoints into a 'GPS route' with the same number as the walking route number; then when you call up the 'GPS route' on Mallorca (West), there should be no confusion as to which walking route it refers,

- repeat the inputting of routes until you have covered all the routes you plan to walk, or until you have used up the memory capacity of your GPS; even the most basic of GPS units will store up to 20 GPS routes of up to 50 waypoints for each route, and you can always re-programme your GPS while on Mallorca,

- turn off your GPS. When you turn the GPS back on it should return to its normal navigation mode.

Personal Navigator Files

Personal Navigator Files are GPS track and waypoint files that cover all the destinations in our current range of Walk! guidebooks, including Walk! Mallorca (West). Both track and waypoint files for walking routes can be downloaded direct to your GPS unit from the PNFs CD using a PC. Your GPS navigation information is transferred in seconds - so much easier than manually inputting waypoints. Current Personal Navigator Files CD Version 2.01 even includes a Special Edition of GPS Utility software with which you can transfer all the track and waypoint information to your gps unit. In addition to all Mallorca (West) GPS information, the Personal Navigator Files CD Version 2.01 includes:

- Alpujarras
- Menorca
- Mallorca (North & Mountains)
- Sierra de Aracena
- La Gomera
- Lanzarote,
- Tenerife
- Madeira
- Andorra
- La Palma

- plus samples of our **UK** walking research so that you test the benefits of GPS navigation in a region near you. Personal Navigator Files CD Version 2.01 £7.99 published 2005 ISBN 1-904946-01-1.

GPS Waypoints are provided as an additional navigation aid to complement the detailed walk descriptions in Walk! Mallorca (West). Knowing exactly where you are in relation to our detailed walk description is a great confidence booster when exploring these new landscapes. GPS Waypoints are provided for all key navigational points on all walking routes; never again should you find yourself wondering whether you are on the right path or not.

Note that GPS Waypoints complement the detailed walking route descriptions, and are not intended for use as an alternative to the route description.

Confused by GPS?

If you are confused by talk of GPS, but are interested in how this modern navigational aid could enhance your walking enjoyment then simply seek out a copy of GPS The Easy Way. Thousands have benefitted from the straight forward explanation of GPS navigation and graded exercises to bring GPS novices up to advanced GPS user status.

"A compass points north."
but
"A GPS tells you where you are, where you've been, and can show you where you want to go."

GPS The Easy Way £4.99 and Personal Navigator Files CD Version 2.01

£7.99 are available from bookshops, outdoors shops, over the internet, and post free from:

Discovery Walking Guides Ltd.
10 Tennyson Close
Northampton NN5 7HJ

More information on GPS The Easy Way and Personal Navigator Files CD is available on our websites:

www.walking.demon.co.uk

www.dwgwalking.co.uk

WALKING EQUIPMENT

Reading the postings on uk.rec.walking internet news group, it is obvious that walkers are very interested in the clothing and equipment used by other walkers. For some this interest borders on obsession, with heated debates over walking poles, boots versus sandals, GPS versus 'map and compass' navigation etc, etc. Walking magazines are packed with clothing and equipment reviews, opinions and adverts, but few walking guide books give more than a cursory mention to recommended clothing and equipment. At the risk of upsetting some walking fundamentalists, here is a brief rundown on what I've used on Mallorca West.

Backpack

A 25-30 litre day pack should easily cope with all the equipment you think you will need for a day's walking. A design with plenty of outside pockets to give easy access to frequently used items, such as ½ litre water bottles, is a good starting point. Well padded straps will spread the load and a waist strap will stop the pack moving about on the more adventurous routes. A ventilated back panel will help clear sweat on hot days and tough routes; a design with a stand-off frame is best for ventilation and worth the small increase in weight. Do spend time adjusting the straps so that you get the most comfortable fit.

As an alternative to traditional backpack designs, you might find the cyclist's packs produced by Nikko, and similar companies, a good compromise of stand-off frame, capacity, pockets and weight.

Footwear

Mallorca West's dramatic landscapes offer no compromises, and nor should you compromise on your footwear. While there are many comfortable paths on the island, a lot of the walking is on hard rock, usually uneven. Whether you choose boots, shoes or sandals they must be up to the task. You will need a hard sole with plenty of grip and a well padded foot-bed. My favourites are a pair of Bestard boots that I picked up at their factory shop on Mallorca. Worn with thick mountain socks, these boots have done everything I have asked of them.

Whichever footwear you choose, do make sure that you have covered plenty of kilometres in them before coming to Mallorca West.

Sun Protection

Always carry a comfortable sun hat, also useful should it rain. Choose a design that gives you plenty of shade, is comfortable to wear, and stays on your head in windy conditions. You will be spending several hours a day outdoors and sunburnt ears (and neck) are both painful and embarrassing. Sunglasses and high-factor sun cream are highly recommended.

Water & Food

Always carry as much water as you think you might drink. A couple of ½ litre bottles, a few pence each from local shops, is the minimum, and add another couple of litres for longer or more strenuous routes. Even on shorter routes, I would advise that you carry some survival rations. While some routes are well equipped with 'tipico' bars, survival rations of chocolate bars and the like can provide welcome comfort.

Medical Kit

Antiseptic wipes, antiseptic cream, plasters and bandage are supplemented by lip salve, which can seem like a life saver in hot dry conditions. Also include tweezers, which you will soon appreciate if you catch a splinter or cactus spine, and a whistle to attract attention if you get into difficulties.

Navigation

Do not compromise - buy the best guide book and the best map, and carry them with you. A compass is useful to orientate yourself at the start of a route and for general directions, but a GPS unit is far more useful - see Using GPS on Mallorca West.

Clothing

Choose loose comfortable clothing and add a lightweight waterproof jacket to your back pack; the Balearics are famous for sunshine but I saw quite a bit of rain while researching this book.

Other Equipment

You won't want to be carrying excess weight during your walking, especially on the longer routes with major ascents/descents. Digital cameras weigh far less than their film equivalents, and a monocular is half the weight of a pair of binoculars. Secateurs might seem an unusual choice of walking equipment, but they may well come in useful on overgrown routes. A mobile phone, and money (refreshments, taxis, public telephones, drinks machines etc.) are also recommended.

1 SERRA DE SON CAMPS : PUJOL DES GAT

Though the **Serra de Son Camps**, a low line of hills defining the junction of the **Valldurgent** and **Puigpunyent** valleys, is virtually unknown to outsiders, it's a little like the local country park for outward bound residents of **Palma**. In the good-old bad-old days, it was a favourite place for dumping obsolete sofas and defunct fridges, but now that the countryside is regarded as a life-enhancing resource rather than an unusually robust rubbish tip, the debris has largely been removed, the tracks have been closed to motorized vehicles, and the only wheels you're likely to see up here will be on a mountain-bike.

The climb to the firewatch tower on **Pujol des Gat** ('The Hillock of the Cat') is a good preliminary excursion, partly because it's very straightforward and can be taken as an uncomplicated test walk, but also because en route we see most of the major peaks and can get the lay of the land for subsequent explorations. If time's short and you want maximum walking for your money, the itinerary can be linked with Walk 2 for a full-day excursion. Look out for wild gladioli and pyramidal orchids (*Anacampsis pyramidalis*) in spring.

Access: by car

The walk starts from km 9.3 of the PMV1016 (**Calvià** to **Establiments**) on a dirt track closed to traffic by metal gates carrying a '*Coto Privado de Caza*' (private hunting) sign. The 300-metre post is on the right behind the fence. Parking's tight here, there's room for two small cars, but larger cars may have to go 500 metres uphill to park safely. If this is the case, note that there's a stretch of dirt track on the right just east of km 8.9 and a path just east of km 9.1 to diminish the road walking.

The gates are locked and lateral fencing blocks access to vehicles on either side, but a well worn route at the eastern end of the fence takes us on to the dirt track (Wp.1 0M), which immediately passes a narrow path climbing to the right. Throughout the ascent, there are several minor branches off the main track, but we ignore them all, and simply turn right at each major junction. The track climbs steadily (ENE), soon bringing the distinctive, triangular summit of **Galatzó** (Walk 22) into view off to our left (NW).

After passing the ragged teeth of a decayed lime-kiln, the track gradually bears right (SSW) and the gradient eases as we climb past a small *aljub* or water-reservoir above the shallow, wooded gorge of **Sa Coma Bella**. The track then levels off amid more varied and healthier woods, interspersed with the abandoned fields of the **Rota de Son Camps** - *rota* being a local word (very local, even people from **Palma** don't always know what it means!) for a mountain smallholding with a cabin rather than a full farmhouse. After passing a broad grassy trail on the right, the track crosses a wall and climbs gently to a narrow cross track (Wp.2 25M) where we bear right.

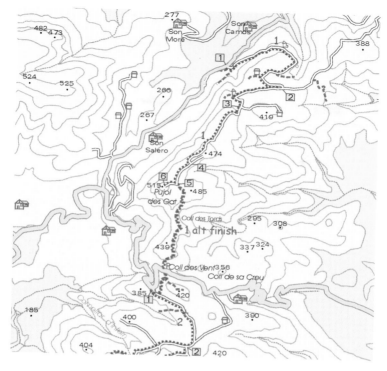

From this track we have more good views of **Galatzó**, to the right of which low cliffs define the summit of **Es Puntals** (Walk 28). The small town below **Es Puntals** is **Puigpunyent** (Walk 29). To the west of **Puigpunyent**, the wooded massif with several large houses near the top is the **Fita del Ram** (Walk 27).

Honeysuckle on the long, level stretch

After a long, level stretch lined with oak, honeysuckle, cistus, and bushy strawberry trees, we pass a second, better preserved lime-kiln. Ignoring a trail branching to the right immediately in front of the lime-kiln, we resume our steady climb to a second major junction (Wp.3 35M), at which point we again bear right.

We now climb onto the main ridge, catching our first glimpse of **Palma** bay. The track climbs, levels and climbs again, bringing into view the firewatch tower on **Pujol des Gat**. Large green gates (unlocked but otherwise easily passable by a breach in the wall on the right) lead to a T-junction (Wp.4 50M), where we take our customary right turn, turning right again a couple of hundred metres later (Wp.5 55M) for the final climb to the top (Wp.6 60M).

Looking to the west of **Galatzó**, we see **S'Esclop** (Walk 21), literally 'The Clog' - not looking especially clog-like from this angle, but you get the picture, with the upturned heel to the left and the sole on the right. Beyond that you can pick out the bare heights of the cliffs behind **Sa Trapa** (Walks 18,19 & 20). The sharp, most distant peak is the tip of **Dragonera** (Walk 17). To the west, long cliffs define the **Garrafa** ridge (Walk 15), and immediately to the south is the bare back of the **Serra de Na Burguesa** (Walks 2 & 3). Between us and **S'Esclop** is the small wooded dome of **Na Bauçana** (Walk 30) and to the left of that, on the nearest ridge, we can see the edge of the **Son Font** *urbanización*, passed in Walk 29. Finally, between **Son Font** and **Na Burguesa**, is the **Valldurgent** valley, visited in Walk 5(d). Identifying all that, let alone walking it, should keep you busy for the rest of your trip.

We return the same way, but if you want to make a full day of it, bear right at Wp.5 and follow the clear trail (rough and steep at first, but soon becoming smoother and less steep) till it ends at the **Coll des Vent** just north of km 6 on the PMV1043 (Wp.7 75M). Ten metres to the left, a trail continues to the south. At the fork 20 metres from the road, turn right on a broad trail descending to join the dirt track fifty metres from the start of Walk 2.

Often neglected by ramblers, the **Serra de na Burguesa** between **Calvià** and **Palma**, is a lovely area for gentle walks with fine views. Though most of the forest along the ridge has been destroyed by decades of fires, the eastern end still boasts some fine pine woodland interspersed with a host of bushy strawberry trees - the red-skinned, orange-fleshed fruit is edible but a bit bland and floury. These woods are also home to a tremendous number of songbirds that conspire in a dawn chorus so intense it sounds like an avian parliament debating a particularly contentious point of order.

Despite the dryness of the highlands, the walk is sufficiently easy to be a pleasant evening excursion during Summer, climbing to the *mirador* for the sunset (take your aperitif!); needless to say, it's equally agreeable as a half-day outing throughout the rest of the year.

Access: by car (alternatively, taxi to the start and turn right at Wp.7 to join Walk 3 at Wp.5)

The walk starts on a green-gated dirt track (Wp.1 0M) at km 6.4 of the PMV-1043, which is marked with kilometre and 100-metre posts, so there's no need to set the odometer. If you have a very small car and a delicate turn of the wrist, there's one parking space beside the gates (do not park in front of the gates as these tracks may be used by firefighting vehicles), otherwise there's more room 150 metres up the road and, beyond that, at the **Coll des Vent** (see Walk 1 for a link path from **Coll des Vent**).

Ignoring a minor branch on the left near the start (alternative access from **Coll des Vent**), we follow the main track, climbing very slightly through attractive woodland with good views of **Galatzó** and **S'Esclop**. The track crosses a belt-and-braces chain against unauthorized motor vehicles and is joined by another track climbing from **Coll de sa Creu**.

Seventy-five metres after the junction, we turn right on a minor branch heading west (Wp.2 15M). Ignoring overgrown branches to left and right a little over five minutes later, we continue in a westerly direction between a dense hedging of strawberry trees. The track then descends to the southwest, crossing a dry watershed, the **Comellar d'Infern**, and passing a lime-kiln (Wp.3 25M), after which it dwindles to a trail.

After climbing across a sparsely forested rise, the trail levels out above **Pla d'en Palem** and follows a contour line round **Puig d'en Bou**, crossing land devastated by forest fires and now almost exclusively colonized by cistus, *Pistacia lentiscus*, and asphodels.

Superb views of S'Esclop and Galatzó from the *mirador*

At a junction (Wp.4 35M) within sight of **Cap Andritxol** (Walk 9) and the telecommunications masts and turquoise firewatch tower above **Vilarrassa**, we maintain a westerly direction to the ruined cabin at the **Mirador de n'Alzamora** (Wp.5 45M), from where we have superb views of the high peaks to the north and the bucolic plain behind the coast.

Retracing our steps to Wp.4, we bear right to circle **Puig d'en Bou**. The path descends slightly before curving east and dropping down to cross another dry watershed, after which a gentle, southerly climb on a gradually broadening trail brings us to a T-junction with a track into the **Coma de n'Aliga** (Wp.6 65M).

Turning left, we climb to a second T-junction, this time with the main track along the ridge (Wp.7 75M). Turning left again, we cross **Coll d'es Pastors**, ignoring two tracks branching off to the right. Defined by sheets of gladioli, the main track climbs along the southern side of **Puig d'en Bou**, levelling off after five minutes at a rare vantage point taking in almost the entire length of the **Tramuntana**, from **S'Esclop** in the west to **Massanella** in the east. We now simply follow the main track through a long gentle descent, rejoining our outward route at Wp.2 (100M).

3 NA BURGUESA: TOUR OF PUIG GROS DE BENDINAT

Our second itinerary on the **Na Burguesa** gives access to this delightful ridge for those without private transport. The start and end involve rather wearing road walking, but otherwise the entire itinerary is a pleasure: easy walking on rocky tracks with great views of **Galatzó**, **S'Esclop**, and an expanse of sea that's nothing less than a symphony in blue. It's a dry and exposed climb, so not recommended in hot weather, but perfect for a clear, fresh, blustery day. To visit the **Mirador de n'Alzamora**, turn left at Wp.5, joining Walk 2 at Wp.7.

*on the coast

Access:
On foot from
**Palmanova/
Portals Nou**

Shorter Circular Option
Motorists can enjoy a shorter circular walk avoiding most of the urbanisations. Drive to Wp.2, and then follow the main walk to the junction at Wp.6 where we follow the track signed 'Costa d'en Blanes' back to Alt waypoint, just fifty metres from our car.

The walk starts from the C719 at the Marineland bus-stop (Lines 103, 106, 107, & 109) on the border between **Palmanova** and **Portals Nou**, where a large roundabout is ornamented with an old steam-engine (Wp.1 0M). We take the **Costa d'en Blanes** road, climbing past the **Saint Michel** apartments and crossing the motorway, seventy-five metres after which, we turn right into **Carrer Santa l'Avinya**. We follow this road for 750 metres, until it curves sharp left, climbing more steeply, and we turn right on a dirt track, the **Camí de Santa l'Avinya** (Wp.2 20M). You may wish to taxi to this point to avoid the road walking.

The track runs parallel to the motorway for 50 metres before swinging left at a junction with a minor track (Alt), after which it climbs steadily alongside the **Costa d'en Blanes** *urbanización*. Hereon in, the itinerary is very simple and, if you don't care to be reading while you're walking, all you need to remember is: up to the top, turn right, along the top, turn right, down to the bottom - all on dirt tracks until the end when we take a clearly signposted path.

The track soon curves away from the uppermost houses of the *urbanización*, fine views opening out over the azure blue sea and up toward the ridge, while the racket of the motorway fades to a distant hum. The rocky western end of **Na Burguesa** comes into view, topped with a turquoise firewatch tower, and the track levels out briefly as it passes an electricity pylon (Wp.3 45M), after which we wind through a double chicane, bringing the main ridge into view. After climbing across land devastated by forest fires but already blooming with cistus, mastic bushes and gladioli, we see **Galatzó** for the first time and cross a shallow depression, passing a green firefighting reservoir. A final steady climb ends at a T-junction on a bend of the main track along the ridge (Wp.4 55M).

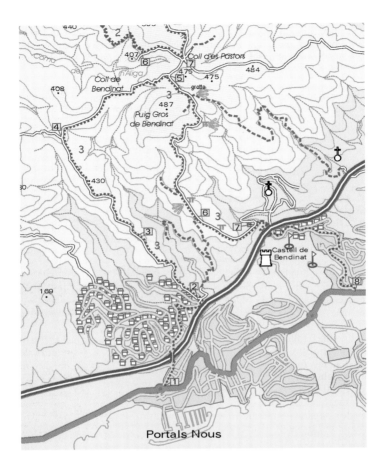

Turning right, we follow the track as it curves round to the east, passing a chain against cars. After crossing the **Coll de Bendinat** (more superb views of **Galatzó**, **Esclop**, and the span of mottled blue to the south), the track climbs behind the rise of **Puig Gros de Bendinat**, where a small area of forest remains intact and the undergrowth has been cleared to preserve it from subsequent brushfires. At a second T-junction (Wp.5 75M), we again turn right, and head south to the gated, signposted start of the **Camí de Bendinat** track.

Soon after the gate and mapboard, we pass an overgrown track on our right and a short signposted path on our left. It's worth following the former for fifty metres or so for views to the east of the high **Tramuntana**, including the **Teix**, the **Alfábia Ridge**, **Puig Major** and **Massanella**. The signpost indicates a fenced viewing point over a deep grotto, also accessible by a narrow, steep path. Subsequent timings allow ten minutes for these two diversions.

Continuing on the main track, we enjoy fine views of the coast between **Palma** and **Andratx**, passing below a couple of benches and a locator board.

There's no real call to be reading a book here, so just carry on down the track, bathing your eyes in blue and keeping watch for a fine herd of wild goats. The track passes two branch paths on our right, the second signposted **Costa d'en Blanes** (Wp.6 110M).

For the present itinerary though, we continue on the **Camí de Bendinat**, passing a couple of picnic tables tucked into the shade of the trees. The track eventually curves round to the east then northeast, at which point we fork right on a path signposted 'Bendinat' (Wp.7 120M).

After a winding descent alongside the **Bendinat** golf course fence, we go through a pedestrian tunnel under the motorway, 100 metres east of **Castell de Bendinat**. If you want a closer look at the castle, turn right after the tunnel, otherwise turn left, crossing two tall ladder stiles just above the tenth green of the golf course to join the end of a tarmac road.

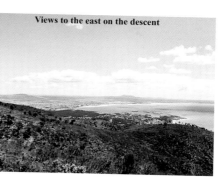
Views to the east on the descent

After the stiles, follow the road (**Carrer del Julio Cortazar** if you happen to be looking for it in the other direction) to the junction with **Avenguida de Mallorca**, the main road climbing through the golf club *urbanización*. Bearing right and ignoring all turn-offs, we follow the main road (briefly called **Camí de la Serra** but generally **Avenguida de Mallorca**) all the way (and I mean *all* the way - after a while you begin to wish the rich could cultivate a passion for billiards or darts or something similarly economical of space) round the golf course, down to join the C719 at the 'Bendinat 2' symbol, next to the **Bendinat Golf** bus-stop (Wp.8 150M).

Bit of a curate's egg this one, in that it's composed of diverse parts - except that unlike the egg in the Punch cartoon, all the parts are good: a succession of idyllic coves so perfect they provided the location for the 1960s film of John Fowles' metaphysical thriller, The Magus; Mallorca's 'other' cathedral, the marble quarry caves that provided the building blocks for the better known version in **Palma**; a scattering of natural caves said to have been inhabited 2000 years ago; an abandoned military camp enjoying the sort of dominant position that was, in less democratic times, the preserve of soldiers, bandits and seabirds; and above all a superb meandering ramble along isolated cliff tops that can only be reached on foot. The route is more complicated than it looks, but simpler than it sounds.

N.B. The **Cap de Cala Figuera** military zone has been abandoned and is open to hikers and cyclists; the **Rafeubetx** military zone is not and is sufficiently emphatic about the prohibition as to deter even pioneering ramblers.

* at **Playa del Mago**

Access: by car and bus

The walk begins from **Casino Mallorca** near **Cala Falcó**. The casino is signposted from the western entrance to **Magaluf** and has a huge, generally empty car-park. Motorists could also follow the **Cala Portals Vells** signs, then turn left for **Playa el Mago**, though cautionary notices suggest this option is more popular with thieves than drivers. The itinerary starts in front of the casino at the **Cala Falcó**, **Avinguda Mallorca**, 84 bus-stop (Line 107).

From the bus-stop (Wp.1 0M), we follow **Avinguda Mallorca** (S), passing **Club Balear** and bearing left at the junction with **Carrer La Ribera**. Opposite **Carrer Monte Alegre**, we turn right on a dirt track descending into a deep valley shrouded with tall eucalyptus and pine, where the track dwindles to a trail. Fifty metres after a large bushy fig tree, we turn right on a slip path (Wp.2 10M) crossing the first of the four **Cala Portals Vells** beaches, from where we can already see the quarry caves on the far side of the bay.

Climbing away from the first beach on a concrete and dirt track, we pass the **Playa el Mago** parking area (optional starting point for drivers) and descend to the beach and restaurant of the same name, climbing steps at the end of the restaurant terrace onto a concrete platform. Taking the path to the left, we follow the coastline, then descend across a succession of broad rock shelves before curving round to the main beach (Wp.3 25M). We then cross a rocky rise to the last tiny beach, from where a clear path leads along the headland to the quarry-caves (Wp.4 30M).

The comparison of these caves with a 'cathedral' is not merely authorial fancy, but one clearly drawn by the sixteenth century quarrymen, who carved altars and a chapel into the caves they had excavated. And, with an eye to dangers more immediate than damnation, they also hollowed out a one-room

'fort', still just visible on the tiny, ragged peninsula in front of the first cave entrance, in which they took refuge from pirates. Allow ten to fifteen minutes (not counted in subsequent timings) for exploring the caves.

The Quarry-Caves

Directly behind the 'fortified' peninsula, we scramble onto gently shelving rocks and pick up a narrow path climbing south for 100 metres to a very short dirt track forking off a tarmac road. From the turning circle at the eastern end of the track (Wp.5 35M), we take a broad way (S) dotted with the remains of campfires and a mosaic of glittering glass fragments from broken bottles. To begin with there's no single path through the scrub, just a series of easy ways meandering along five to ten metres behind the cliffs. After crossing the dead-end of a slip road a couple of minutes later, red and mustard waymarks indicate our route across slabs of limestone hemmed in by shrubs, wild olive and pine. Blue waymarks appear as the path becomes clearer, bringing the lighthouse and abandoned military buildings on **Cap de Cala Figuera** into view. We bear left at a junction with a broad trail then, three minutes later and thirty metres before the trail ends above the tiny inlet of **Cala en Beltran**, turn right on a narrow path picked out with bright blue waymarks (Wp.6 50M).

Forking left twenty metres later, we follow the blue-waymarked path as it skirts behind **Cala en Beltran** then crosses the rocky scrubland north of **Cala Figuera**. The tiny caves seen on the far side of the creek as we curve into **Cala**

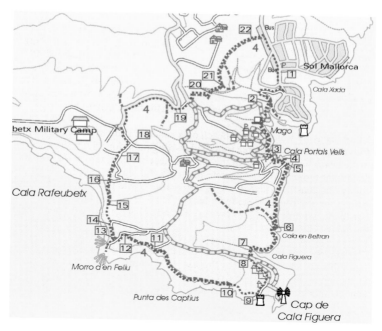

Figuera, are the ones said to have been inhabited 2000 years ago. The path swings right, crosses a hump of rock then descends past the clean cut walls of a small quarry. A waymarked route then winds across rocks, some care required here, passing in front of a small cave before descending to the beach (Wp.7 65M), which is idyllic but sadly cluttered with masses of jetsam.

On the far side of the beach, a blue waymark and two steps cut into the rock lead us onto the southern side of the *cala*. At a Y-junction below the first shallow overhang cave, we turn right, taking a waymarked, partially stepped route up to the lighthouse/military zone road (Wp.8 70M). Turning left and ignoring the *prohibido el paso* signs, we follow the road into the military zone, passing several abandoned buildings and a couple of gun emplacements, then bear right on a dirt track leading to the precarious remains of a sixteenth century watchtower (Wp.9 80M).

From the watchtower, we head west, once again on an easy but pathless way meandering along 5-10 metres behind the cliffs, overlooking deep inlets defined by walls of sheer yellow rock. Joining a clear path (Wp.10 90M), we continue meandering through delightfully peaceful scrubland before curving inland at a much wider but unnamed inlet between the **Punta des Captius** and **Morro d'en Feliu** headlands.

The path becomes more obscure here, but sticking to the main way and looking out for occasional cairns, we join a dirt track at the point where it dwindles to a trail (Wp.11 110M). Bearing left, we follow the trail, which in turn dwindles to a path leading to a second dirt track, where we again turn left (Wp.12 115M). After two or three minutes, we pass the junction with our return route, a major trail to the right (Wp.13), but first we follow the track onto the **Morro d'en Feliu**, where it splinters into three natural *miradors* overlooking the immense **Cala Rafeubetx**, behind which lies the second military zone.

Returning to the junction of trail and track (Wp.13 125M), we bear left (NW) and follow the trail as it tapers to a narrow path winding between the pine to the end of another dirt track (Wp.14 130M). We bear right and, when the track curves sharp right 50 metres later, turn left on a rough way that soon loses definition in the rocks behind the cliffs.

The spur-thighed tortoise

There's no path here, but goat droppings 'waymark' the obvious route and the 5-10 metre cliff rule holds as we follow the line of the **Rafeubetx** bay - we saw a spur-thighed tortoise here, so keep your eyes peeled. Climbing gently in a northerly direction, we join a clearer, cairn-marked path (Wp.15 140M).

Sticking to the cairn-marked route at several faint junctions, we soon cross the end of another broad dirt track, the second since the **Morro d'en Feliu** (Wp.16 150M), within sight of two clifftop bunkers overlooking **Cala**

Rafeubetx, about 500 metres from the easternmost bunker.

Fifty metres after the track, we fork right on the cairn-marked path (NNE), away from the military zone on the **Rafeubetx** heights, through an area carpeted with orchids in spring. Three minutes later, we join a third track leading (N) to a broad sandy clearing (Wp.17 155M). If you miss the fork and find yourself confronted with the curled barbed wire fence of the military zone, follow the fence north until a broad trail branching right leads back to the sandy area at Wp.17.

Paths and trails and apparent paths and false trails head off in every direction here. Ignore them all and stay on the track as it swings round to the right, passing a minor dirt track doubling back to the left. At a junction with a major track roughly stabilized with stones (Wp.18 160M), we turn left, joining the **Rafeubetx** military zone access road three minutes later at a T-junction in front of a 'Ministerio de Defensa' sign painted on the backdrop colours of a Spanish flag. Turning right, we follow this roughly surfaced road (ENE), passing a couple of branch tracks and walking alongside a 'gapped' wall.

After a while the military road descends slightly and swings north toward its junction with the **Cala Portals Vells** road. Immediately after the bend, a vivid orange waymark on the corner of one of the walls (Wp.19 175M) marks the point where we leave the military road, turning right on a very faint path leading to a dirt track 10 metres away. Turning left, we follow this track for 100 metres down to the junction of the roads to **Cala Portals Vells** and **Playa el Mago**, where we have a choice of routes. For simplicity, sea, parking and food, follow the **Playa El Mago** road down to rejoin our outward route a few minutes south of Wp.2. For a roundabout woodland stroll back to the casino, turn left ten metres down the **Playa El Mago** road on an initially litter-strewn dirt trail.

The trail soon cleans up its act and curves east, descending into a shallow valley before disappearing in a ploughed almond grove (Wp.20 185M). Bearing right, we cross the almond grove to the first and lowest of two obvious breaches in its eastern wall. After crossing the wall, we turn sharp left, following red and white bulls-eye waymarks up steeply sloping rocks to join a narrow path. At a T-junction (Wp.21 190M), we again turn left, following the bulls-eye waymarks. Ignoring all branches, we now simply follow this waymarked path through the woods until it emerges behind the **Urbanización Pinar del Sol 3** (Wp.22 205M) apartment complex. Crossing the complex via the driveway to the left and taking the walkway underneath apartments 3-11 and 3-12, we emerge on **Avinguda de Mallorca**. The **Cala Falcó**, **Avinguda Mallorca**, N°50 bus-stop is fifty metres to our left, the casino three hundred metres on the right.

Calvià *ayuntamiento* has recently signposted a series of attractive rural tracks deemed suitable as walking trails and bridleways. Unfortunately, none of them can be incorporated into a discrete, coherent, non-trespassing rambling route! Hence this catch-all itinerary detailing a few of the *camís*.

None of these itineraries should be regarded as a full-scale walk. They are simply pleasant country strolls, sundowners and lunch-downers, suitable for working up an appetite on a summer's evening or digesting the midday meal during winter. They all involve easy walking on clear dirt tracks and little-used lanes hidden away in the delightful countryside around **Calvià** and **Capdella**.

(a) Camí de la Vall Verda

1	1H	4.5 km	100m	(one way)	3*

*in **Capdella**

Access: by bus

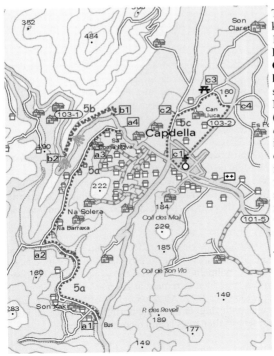

This stroll starts at km 3.4 of the PMV-1012 (**Capdella** to **Peguera**) at the **Capdella, Camí de la Vall Verda** bus-stop (line Circular Norte N°110) (Wp.A1 0M). The *camí* starts immediately south of the bus-stop and is very easy to follow, as we simply stay on the main track all the way except for one signposted junction.

To begin with, the track is very broad and a bit bleak as it follows the **Torrent de Sa Coma** (also known as **Torrent d'es Gore**), but after a little over five minutes, it narrows to more tempting rambling dimensions and the 'green valley' begins to earn its name as we climb gently between fields of sparse, spindly grasses spotted with wild flowers.

After dipping down to cross and re-cross the dry torrent, we see the great grey and orange cliffs of the **Garrafa** plateau and the track curves west to a signposted Y-junction (Wp.A2 20M) where we turn right for **Capdella**. Climbing across a small rise, we pass the **Comellar de Na Barraxa** smallholding. The track then runs alongside the shallow **Na Solera** valley, lined with a succession of cabins, huts and cottages in various states of disrepair.

After passing the nicely restored house of **Sa Coma Nova** (Wp.A3 40M), the track curves round to join the **Capdella-Andratx** road, the PMV-1031 (Wp.A4 45M). From here we can either walk up the road for 100 metres to the start of option (b), or turn right and follow the road down to **Capdella**.

Sa Coma Nova, Wp.A3

(b) Camí Vell d'es Capdella a Andratx (sic)

** plus 1-2 kilometres if walking from **Capdella**
* in **Capdella**

Access: on foot from **Capdella** or as an extension to option (a)

This stroll starts 500 metres west of the **Capdella** city-limits sign (800 metres from the centre) on a bend in the PMV-1031 to **Andratx** (Wp.B1 0M). Turning right at the gap in the fence 15 metres behind the mapboard, we head NE for 75 metres, after which the track veers left and dwindles to a path, which we simply follow all the way to the location board at its end (Wp.B2 15M).

It's a pleasant path, enjoying fine views south over **Vall Verda** and east toward **Capdella**, and has been fixed with stumpy posts identifying classic flora and fauna: wild olive, palmetto, carob, and the spur-thighed tortoise, only the last of which has neglected to remain at his post. Unfortunately, it joins the new road six kilometres from **Andratx**, so its official title is a bit cheeky. There are various paths higher up to the north, but they've all been abandoned and are so beset by fallen trees I can't recommend them.

We return by the same path.

(c) Camí del Graner del Delme

Access: on foot from **Capdella**   *in **Capdella**

Galatzo, as seen on walk (c)

From the *ayuntamiento* in **Capdella** (Wp.C1 0M), we take **Carrer de Galatzó** to the north, soon coming into view of the street's towering eponym. We stroll between old houses and fields full of wild flowers then, immediately after house No.48, turn right on the **Camí del Graner del Delme** (Wp.C2 10M).

The track winds between almond groves, passing a small picnic table and multilingual information board about the **Delme Granary**. Immediately after the signboard we fork right (Wp.C3 15M) (the left hand fork is signposted 'Galilea/Puigpunyent', a somewhat generous definition of a track that leads to the **Galilea** road a few hundred metres later!) to join the PMV-1032 (Wp.C4 20M), which we follow back to the village.

(d) Camí de Son Boronat

*** 1 hour 40 min (linear return), 1 hour 20 min (returning to Calvià via the PMV-1016)

** 7 km (linear return), 5.5 km (returning to Calvià via the PMV-1016)

* in **Calvià**

Access: by bus

The **Camí de Son Boronat** starts 200 metres north of the junction of the PMV-1015 (Calvià-Palmanova) and PMV-1014 (Calvià-Santa Ponca) at a bus-stop (Wp.D1 0M) (Lines 110 & 111) cunningly named 'Calvià'(!), however the bus drivers should know the name of the *camí*.

We follow the signposted lane between almond and olive groves and fields of wheat dotted with the occasional asphodel, ignoring all branches until we come to a clear fork (Wp.D2 10M). Bearing right on a partially surfaced track, we pass spacious orchards of lemon and medlar trees, after which life gets a bit boisterous below two well-fenced households with very large, very loud dogs.

After **Son Torrens**, things calm down considerably as the **Valldurgent** valley opens out to our left and the **Na Burguesa** ridge rises above us on the right. Crossing a small rise, we see **Can Boronat** in the distance. We then pass a large solitary eucalyptus tree (Wp.D3 30M), fifty metres after which we ignore roughly painted arrows that appear to waymark a turning to the left.

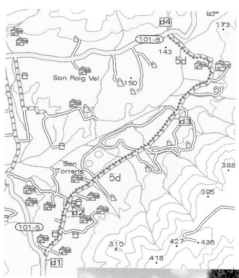

Ten minutes later, the track passes **Son Boronat**, a working farm that also doubles as a hotel/restaurant, after which we curve round WNW before joining the **Valldurgent** road, the PMV-1016 (Wp.D4 50M), 1.5 km from **Calvià**'s city limits, 2 km from the town centre.

Son Boronat

Though there's no wayside, the road is broad and little used apart from cyclists. Otherwise, return to Wp.1 via the same route.

The unreconstructed purist will probably dismiss this infinitely gentle stroll (half of it on tarmac) as a non-walk. If you're a rough-rock, "Ooh-look-at-the-drop, Mind-that-eagle's-nest" rambler, steer clear. If, on the other hand, phrases like 'quiet country lane', 'easy walking', 'bucolic landscape' and 'peaceful countryside' elicit a lively flush of anticipation, then this is the walk for you.

Access: on foot from **Calvià**.   *in **Santa Ponça**

We start at the western end of **Calvià** on **Avinguda d'es Capdella** at the **Carrer de ca na Cucó** bus-stop (Wp.1 0M), fifty metres west of which, we fork left on **Carrer de Pontet**, also signposted 'cementeri'. Two hundred metres later, having passed the fine old house of **Es Pontet**, we again fork left for *cementeri*, then left again seventy-five metres later on the **Camí de Son Pillo** (Wp.2 5M). And that's all you really need to know as the rest of the route simply follows this lane till a signposted path on the right leads to a lovely streamside bridleway down to **Santa Ponça**.

After traversing an area of scattered housing and several paddocks, the **Camí de Son Pillo** passes another fine old house, **Can Estades**, and runs into open countryside. Ignoring a minor fork to the right, we stay on the main lane as it crosses rolling fields dotted with almond and fig trees, passing the **Camí d'es Molí Nou** to **Capdella** and the **Son Malero** lane back to **Calvià**. The **Camí de Son Pillo** then dips down very slightly, passing between some tall pine, and we turn right just before an abandoned electricity transformer tower, on a path signposted **Santa Ponça** (Wp.3 35M).

The path almost immediately crosses the **Santa Ponça** stream and passes a mapboard announcing the start of the **Camí d'es Barranc de Santa Ponça**, a delightful bridleway running alongside the stream between wild olive, honeysuckle, *pistacia lentiscus*, cistus and a riot of wild flowers.

... a small but distinctive mouth of rock ...

A little over five minutes later, the main trail crosses onto the left bank of the stream, passing below a small but distinct mouth of rock. We then return to the right bank for a couple of hundred metres before crossing the stream for the last time.

The trail winds between sheets of bamboo before coming to a superb stand of poplar, the silvery undersides of their leaves whispering in the breeze, where we pass a couple of shady picnic tables (Wp.4 55M). It then gradually broadens to the width of a track and we pass three branches off to the left before going through gates within sight of a ruined mill reminiscent of a piece of modern sculpture.

After passing two more branches on the left, we come to a second mapboard just short of the C719 (Wp.5 75M), where we can either bear left to the new footbridge over the road, or (as mapped) turn right to go under the road via the watercourse tunnels, immediately after which we bear left on a narrow path running alongside a large wheat field.

At the end of the field, we turn left alongside a new road (under construction May 2004) leading to the large roundabout at the entrance to **Santa Ponça**, where we turn right for the **Avinguda del Rey Jaume I** bus-stops in front of the **Caprabo** supermarket (Wp.6 90M).

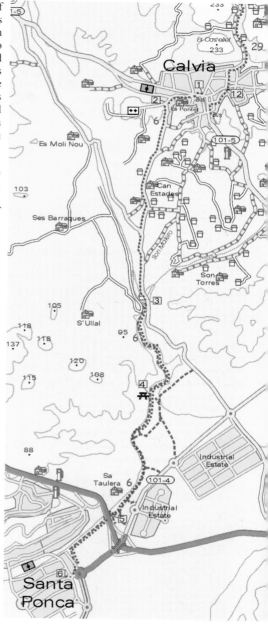

This short, easy walk is ideal for stretching your legs on a summer's evening or, conversely, getting a blast of sea air on a stormy winter's day. Don't be deceived by the house-hugging track on the map: the first stretch is a delightful stroll through pleasant countryside, and the wildness of the **Ribellet** headland is quite astonishing, given its proximity to so many villas.

1 | 1½ H | 7 km | 100m / 100m | 2*

*in **Santa Ponça**

Access: on foot from **Santa Ponça** (**Cala de ses Penyes Rotges/Port Adriano**).

The walk starts at the **Penyes Rotges/El Toro** bus-stop (TIB Lines, N°s 104, 105 & 109, Transabus Lines, N°s L2 & L10) at the southern end of **Santa Ponça**, next to the **Port Adriano** turn-off. From the bus-stop (Wp.1 0M), we follow the **Magaluf** road (SE) to a large roundabout (Wp.2), where we turn right, toward a '*zona verde*' sign and blank mapboard flanking a long, stony track.

Ignoring the no-entry sign (aimed at cars rather than ramblers), we follow the long, straight track between the **El Toro** *urbanizaciónes* and the large flat field of **Pla de ses Penyes Rotges**, with clouds of swallows swooping overhead and a cacophony of songbirds thronging the treetops.

After a little over ten minutes easy strolling, the track climbs slightly, amid healthy young pine gradually curving away from the last scattered villas before running alongside a road. After fifty metres, track and road diverge and we turn right through the pillars of a gateway (Wp.3 25M), to the signposted start of an old concrete stairway descending to a long destroyed landing.

Racó de sa Fragata

Even if you don't take the stairs, it's worth coming this far as the view along the headland to **Illa del Toro** is superb. However, I recommend descending, as the spectacular stepped path opens out views of some lovely, partially submerged rock formations and the toe-curling cliffs of **Racó de sa Fragata**.

When the steps turn sharp right at the bottom for the final descent through a narrow cutting, a rocky path branches off to the left. It's worth following this path for five minutes to see more closely the yellow-legged herring gulls that consider this their own personal kingdom. We then retrace our steps to

Wp.3 and continue along the stony track. Allow twenty-five minutes return for this diversion.

Continuing along the stony track, we soon come to the gated entrance of an abandoned military zone. Military zones can often be crossed when not in use, but given that this one is double-fenced with barbed wire, has coils of the stuff tangled between the two lines of fencing, and the odd protruding spike, I have half a suspicion the prohibition on entry is intended seriously. Fortunately a reasonable path skirts the fence to the left, winding between cistus, *pistacia lentiscus*, and gladioli.

The path soon curves away from the fence, joining another faint forest path at a junction marked by two cairns (Wp.4 60M). It is possible to continue alongside the fence, but it becomes increasingly overgrown and is a laced with discarded scraps of rusty barbed wire, so we turn left and follow the path as it meanders through the woods, deviating occasionally to skirt fallen trees.

After a while we see **Cap d'es Llamp** then, as we descend, **S'Esclop** and **Galatzó** off to our right, after which we reach a T-junction behind the wall defining the stony track (Wp.5 70M). We turn right here, then left fifty metres later, rejoining our outward route via a breach in the wall.

Sa Bruta is the rocky ridge between **Peguera** and the C719 **Túnel de Son Vich**. The path itself is not especially interesting, but the views from the summit of **Es Castellot de na Marío** are superb, taking in the entire coast between **Cap d'es Llamp** and **Magaluf**, the **Garrafa** ridge, the mountains behind **Sant Elm**, and the summits of **S'Esclop** and **Galatzó**. Ideal for the first day if you're based in or around **Peguera**. After Wp.3, the ascent is very well marked with cairns.

| 3 | 1H 35M | 5.5 km | ∧∧∧ | 250m ↑ / 250m ↓ | ↻ | ⚠ | 3* |

*in **Peguera**

Access: on foot from **Peguera**.

The walk starts at the western end of **Peguera**, on the northern side of the **Cala Fornells** roundabout, diagonally opposite the **Casa Pepe** supermarket, and begins with a steady climb through the swathe of villas behind **Peguera**. Setting off on **Carrer de la Talaia** (Wp.1 0M), we take the third turning on the left, **Carrer Dr. Noe** (Wp.2), then fork right fifty metres later on **Carrer Tamarinde**. We then bear right on **Calle Bellavista**, which continues as **Carrer de Baladre**, passing the **Monte Esmeralda** flats, beyond which the road ends in a turning circle (Wp.3 20M).

Continuing on a stony track through the gates of an abandoned *urbanización* project, we climb toward a small stone ruin, forty metres short of which we bear right on a broad trail marked with cairns (Wp.4). Following the cairns, we climb gently to steadily amid scattered, scorched pine, and large bushes of cistus, *pistacia lentiscus* and broom, with fine views over the **Ensenada de Santa Ponça**, passing en route a cairn-marked path on our left (Wp.5 30M) (part of the alternative return route). The trail gradually curves round the mountain, bringing the hinterland into view, after which we turn sharp left, leaving the broad trail and taking a clear path flanked by cairns (Wp.6 35M).

Looking east, before the first rocky outcrop

Fifty metres later, at a junction of paths marked by a large cairn, we bear right (Wp.7 the path directly ahead is also part of the alternative return) and climb steadily to steeply, passing junctions with two more faint paths (SW & NE), shortly after which we come to a large outcrop of rock.

Ignoring a cairn to the right, we can either scramble directly over this outcrop, or skirt round to its left on a rough way strewn with felled trees. In either case,

The final ascent

on the far side we recover a clear path and see the craggy summit of **Es Castellot de na Marío** fifty metres to the north. The path winds into the base of the rocks before curving into a final easy, but slightly vertiginous (slightly more so in descent!) ledge leading to the top (Wp.8 40M), from where we have superb views through 360°.

The return is generally done by the same route, but if you wish to extend the walk a little, there are two alternative paths. Whatever you do though, take care on the ledge descent, especially when it's wet.

Alternative returns

The first alternative begins at the junction of paths marked with a large cairn (Wp.7). The path to the south west follows a contour line before curving back to rejoin our outward route thirty metres above Wp.5. The path to the south-west from Wp.5 also loops through the woods before joining a logging track (Wp.9 60M) fifty metres behind the stone ruin seen earlier. From here we can either turn left to recover our outward route or turn right and follow the track, which immediately dwindles to a broad trail, descending through the woods to the southwest.

This trail eventually emerges on the wide and, at this point, virtually unused **Carrer Bonavida** (Wp.10 75M) behind the brick red, pale pink and beige apartments (not nearly so appalling as they sound!) of **Hotel Don Antonio**.

Turning left, we follow the road behind the apartments and down past the hotel. When **Carrer Bonavida** swings right at the **Complejo Residencial La Colina** (Wp.11), we carry straight on, following **Carrer del Bosc** until it curves into **Carrer Llimonara** (Wp.12). Bearing right shortly after the 'zona verde' signs (Wp.13), we return to the centre of **Peguera** via **Carrer de l'Olivera**.

As a rule we avoid itineraries where access is contested, but a walk that is also a *cause celebre* and a modern fairy tale is hard to resist. Fragrant from her days wafting up and down the catwalk, Beauty (in the shape of supermodel, Claudia Schiffer) was disinclined to have beastly sweaty ramblers tramping all over her newly purchased retreat on **Cap Andritxol**, so she installed a fence along her boundary, neatly segmenting the serpentine path to the **Torre de Andritxol** watchtower. Sadly, Beauty had misjudged the Beast if she thought ramblers could be so readily deterred. As far as Mallorcan walkers were concerned, it was out with the wire-cutters and on with the TV cameras, as a result of which, Beauty bowed to the Beast and the path remains open, scarred by an ugly fence, but open nonetheless, and is used by dozens of tourists every day.

The end of the line.

Version (a), Courting Claudia, follows one of the traditional routes to the watchtower, running the entire length of the disputed fence. This version may change slightly as there is a rumour Ms. Schiffer is prepared to pick up the tab for a new path alongside her fence. Meanwhile, walkers with acute qualms about property boundaries, may prefer **Version (b), Softly, Softly, the (almost) uncontested route**. I say 'almost' because there's a short stretch where we have to stray onto the 'wrong' side of the fence, but it's sufficiently far from the house to reassure even the most reticent rambler.

The walk is 'softly, softly' in that it avoids potential confrontation, but there's nothing soft about the <u>very</u> energetic climb, which would make a treacherous descent in wet weather.

(a) Courting Claudia - the traditional route

| 2 | 2½ H | 8.5 km | ⋀⋀ 200m / 200m | ↻ | 3* |

*in **Peguera**

Access: on foot from **Peguera**

Like the preceding itinerary, this walk begins at the western end of **Peguera**, next to the **Cala Fornells** roundabout and the **Casa Pepe Supermarket**. In this instance though, we start on the southern side of the roundabout, at the junction of roads to the left of the supermarket, where there's a taxi stand, a profusion of signposts advertising hotels and restaurants, and a more demure stone sign for **Cala Fornells** (Wp.1 0M). Our path begins directly behind the signs, climbing through the woods to the right. Almost immediately we encounter a maze of crisscrossing paths, but maintaining direction (WSW)

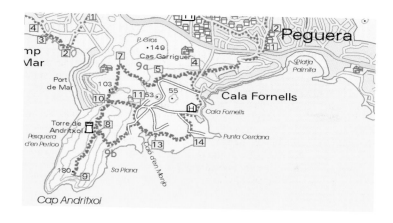

parallel to the road behind the supermarket, we soon cross the road when it doubles back at a U-bend (Wp.2).

We then bear left, following the main path, which is waymarked with faint red dots, forking right fifty metres later and crossing a broad dirt trail. At the next major junction (Wp.3), we fork right again, descending slightly to a bend in an old road, now little more than a dirt track. Bearing left, we cross the new **Cala Fornells** road just below a cutting (Wp.4 15M), already in sight of the *torre*. We are now on the peninsula proper and, if you don't feel like having your nose buried in a book, you can simply wander as instinct suggests. Otherwise…

Ignoring a major fork to the left 50 metres from the road, we follow a broad trail flanked by broom, lavender and *pistacia lentiscus*. This soon joins a major trail climbing from **Cala Fornells** (Wp.5 20M), which in turn leads to another junction a minute later. Forking left we climb gently across bare, sandy coloured rock to another major junction (Wp.6). Turning right then right again at the next junction, we continue climbing (NW) to reach a first breach in the infamous fence (Wp.7 30M). If all that sounds baffling, the fifteen minutes between the road and the fence can be simplified (including the Wp.5 junction) as: right, right, left, right, right.

We now simply turn left and follow the path crisscrossing the course of the fence and climbing steadily to the **Torre de Andritxol** (Wp.8 60M) each making their own personal choice about whether to follow the path on the western side of the fence (Claudia's side) or the undisputed eastern side when there's an option - in fact, there's only one stretch where this is impossible. The *torre*, built as a watchtower to warn against marauding pirates, is on Claudia's side of the fence.

Our next objective are the cliffs at the tip of the headland. It is possible to head directly south from the tower, but it's easier to cross back onto the eastern side via a hole under the fence thirty metres beyond the tower. Again, the path crisscrosses the fence as it meanders along the rocky headland, eventually passing a small windbreak to reach the abrupt and very precipitous **Andritxol** cliffs (Wp.9 70M). If you don't like heights, hang back to enjoy the superb sea views and, in spring, the tremendous display of wild flowers on the **Camp de Mar** side of the peninsula.

Caló d'en Monjo

We now retrace our steps past the tower to the third cutting encountered in the fence on the way up (Wp.10 90M), from where the main trail descends to the east, soon passing the remains of an old lime-kiln. At the first major crossroads (Wp.11 100M), we turn right and descend to cross a major dirt track just above the idyllic little creek of **Caló d'en Monjo**.

To reach the creek itself, we traverse the walled land of an abandoned private property, then bear left along the lowermost, coastal wall, where steps lead down to the water's edge (Wp.12 105M).

To return to **Peguera**, we take the narrow path through the woods on the northern side of the creek, where it crosses a breach in a wall to join a broad trail (N.B. before crossing the wall, a faint path leading round the headland offers superb views over the creek and the water-cave on its southern side). Fifty metres from the breach in the wall (Wp.13), we fork left and, after passing a linking track between the two tines of the fork, bear right at a T-junction, then immediately fork left. When the track crosses a hump of earth, we turn left on a major dirt track (Wp.14) leading to a mapboard (Wp.15 120M) just above **Cala Fornells**.

Turning right, we descend past the **Hotel Petit Cala Fornells** to the coast road (Wp.16) through **Cala Fornells**, either catching the bus from the stop above the first inlet, or following the road past the next inlet before turning left on **Carretera de Cala Fornells** (Wp.17) to rejoin our outward route just below the cutting at Wp.4.

(b) Softly, Softly - the (almost) uncontested route

* in **Peguera**

Access: on foot from **Cala Fornells**

The walk starts from the bus-stop (Lines N°s109 & 110) at the end of the **Cala Fornells** road. From the bus-stop (Wp.1 0M), we walk up the last stretch of tarmac, passing the entrance to **Hotel Petit Cala Fornells**, after which we continue on dirt track. When the main track bears left in front of a mapboard (Wp.2 & Wp.15 of Version (a)), we maintain direction (W) on a broad track

gated against cars by a sturdy wooden barrier.

Ignoring three branches on the right, one signposted **Camp de Mar/Andritxol**, and a branch on the left, we stick to the main track as it curves behind **Caló d'en Monjo**, passing the entrance to an abandoned private property, where we again intersect with Version (a). When the track descends on the southern side of the creek, we branch right, maintaining direction (SW) on a broad trail signposted **Andritxol** (Wp.3 15M).

The trail climbs gently at first, then steepens as it passes a minor branch on the left (Wp.4), climbing steadily with fine views across the bay to the **Illes Malgrat**. After a long zigzag, the trail ends on a small spur (Wp.5 25M), and we turn sharp right on a rough, rocky path. The path climbs steadily then steeply, rapidly dwindling to a rough 'way' marked by cairns every five or ten metres. After a very steep climb across the rocks, the gradient eases slightly and the cairn-marked way bears right for a final, pathless climb across bare rock, joining the main path along the headland (Wp.6 40M) on the uncontested side of the fence.

Turning left, we reach the fence 75 metres later, fifty metres south of the *torre*, from where we follow the contested version of the walk to the cliffs at the end of the peninsula. We return by the same route, but with the option to cross the abandoned private property behind **Caló d'en Monjo** to join Version (a) (Wps.12 - 15) to meet our outward route at the signboard.

Hate tarmac? Turn the page. Fond of straight lines and logical progress? Give up rambling. Like quiet country lanes, hidden coves, and meandering for meandering's sake? Read on. There's no logic to this walk, nothing's achieved, no object gained, no summit conquered, no viewpoint ticked off the list, but if you feel like an agreeable afternoon's rambling, it's just the ticket.

*** 2 hours 40 mins to **Andratx**, 1 hour 30 mins to **Port Andratx**
**   **Andratx** 250 metres ascents, 0 metres descents
      Port Andratx 150 ascents, 150 metres descents
*   in **Andratx**

Access: on foot from **Camp de Mar** (return on foot, by bus or by taxi)

Starting from the roundabout bus-stop behind **Camp de Mar** (Wp.1 0M) (Lines N°s 100 & 102 & the **Mercado Andratx** bus), we follow **Avinguda de sa Platja** past **Bar El Quijote** and take the pedestrian street down to the seafront (Wp.2). Turning right, we stroll along the promenade until it ends in steeply raked stairs climbing to the PM-102 (Wp.3 10M). Following the road to the left, we skirt the **Bahía Camp de Mar Aparthotel** complex, turning left at a small roundabout (Wp.4), then left again on **Camí de Cala en Cranc** (Wp.5).

Ignoring two cul-de-sacs to the left, we descend to what is at present the end of the road (Wp.6 20M) in front of **Villa Cala en Cranc** (though this may change as the tarmac, currently submerged in mud, curves off to the right). N.B. the road detour to reach this point is not as perverse as it may seem, the coast between the promenade and **Cala en Cranc** having effectively been privatized.

Ignoring the very steep, shallow-stepped concrete 'stairway' directly ahead, we bear right on a cairn-marked path climbing gently through peaceful woodland (WSW) to join an *urbanización* road (Wp.7 25M), **Carrer Gerani**, also accessible by a narrow slip path branching left fifty metres earlier. The conventional, cairn-marked route turns right here, but holding true to the meandering principles of this walk, we turn left on two short detours.

Theatre/Loft at Wp.8

The First Detour

First, fans of contemporary architecture should descend to the end of the road to see house N°20 (Wp.8), Theatre/Loft, a modernist take on a medieval fortress, crossed with a sailing vessel and a climbing wall, and evidently built by someone with a peculiarly filial love for the sea.

Allow ten minutes for this detour (counted in subsequent timings) and be prepared for the neighbour's very large, very loud dog - not at liberty but shockingly noisy.

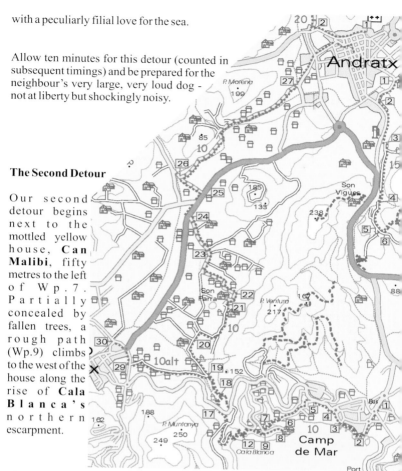

The Second Detour

Our second detour begins next to the mottled yellow house, **Can Malibi**, fifty metres to the left of Wp.7. Partially concealed by fallen trees, a rough path (Wp.9) climbs to the west of the house along the rise of **Cala Blanca's** northern escarpment.

Cala Blanca

When the path joins a second *urbanización* road (Wp.10), **Carrer Gladiol**, just short of house N°31, we turn left then left again thirty metres later (Wp.11), leaving the road to descend a rough path to an old wall overlooking **Cala Blanca** (Wp.12).

Turning right, we follow the wall, crossing it at the second breach, onto an even rougher path descending past the end of the **Cala Blanca** access road to the small beach behind the creek (Wp.13 50M) (N.B. The path down to the beach is very rough and frequently friable; if you don't intend swimming, turn directly onto the access road).

From the beach, we climb an eroded gully (in fact the remains of a dirt track) back to the parking area at the end of the road (Wp.14). Once on the road, we climb through a long U-bend to a junction with another, unnamed road leading to a couple of new villas on **Cap d'es Llamp**. Ten metres along this branch road, just behind a red '11' painted on the kerb (Wp.15), we step over a low wall onto a broad trail climbing through the woods to rejoin the PM-102 near km 1.9 (Wp.16 65M).

As indicated by a pointing-hand signpost, we follow the road to the left for a little over fifty metres then turn right on a footpath (Wp.17) marked by a multilingual sign flimsily attached to the bushes. There are actually two footpaths leaving this road: ours is the second and lies thirty metres after the fire-hazard warning sign, just opposite the km 1.8 kilometre post.

The path, which is well marked with cairns, descends through pleasant woodland, passing a branch to a cabin on the left before following a retaining wall to a junction with another path on the far side of the valley (Wp.18 70M). Turning left, we descend along this path, which gradually broadens to a trail running alongside a wire fence, joining a bend in a dirt track in front of the entrance to house N°27a (Wp.19 75M), where the **Andratx** and **Port Andratx** routes divide.

For Andratx

Turn right (N), descending past a house with a blue lattice gate. Ignoring branch tracks to right and left, we stay on the main track as it curves round to the northeast, passing a sign identifying it as the 'Camí de Sa Vinya' and the entrance to a large private property. Ignoring the major track coming in from the left (Wp.20) and all subsequent branches, including a major branch on the left 100 metres later, we now follow the continuation of the **Camí de sa Vinya**, the **Camí des Ribolls**, as it climbs slightly and passes directly behind a large traditional house, at the entrance to which, it becomes a tarmac lane (Wp.21 95M).

The lane, which is called **Es Girgolar** but not yet signposted as such, curves round a lemon grove below the imposing mansion of **Son Parra** (Wp.22), passing several branch tracks before joining a bend in the **Camí de Coll Baix** (Wp.23). Turning left then left again seventy-five metres later, we descend to the busy main road between **Andratx** and the Port (Wp.24 115M) and the least agreeable stretch of the walk. Fortunately, it only lasts 200 metres.

Crossing onto the far side of the road (quickly, it's an unpleasantly fast road when you're on foot), we walk up the C719 past the **S'Arraco** turning and, seventy-five metres later, in front of the **Es Rieral** farm shop, turn left onto the **Camí de Morella** (Wp.25), thankfully putting the main road behind us. When the lane approaches a give-way sign above the **S'Arraco** road, we turn right (Wp.26), staying on the **Camí de Morella**. We now simply follow this pretty country lane as it climbs gently to **Andratx**, ignoring the senars and parells, odd and even-numbered branch lanes also called 'Camí de Morella'.

After the football ground (Wp.27 145M), we turn left and follow **Calle Aragón** and **Carrer Catalunya** into town. At the end of **Carrer Catalunya**, we turn right on **Calle Pedro A. Pujol**, carrying straight on at the *panaderia* onto **Calle Antonio Calafell** then turning right on the pedestrianized **Via Roma** down to the town's bar-lined central plaza (**Bar C'as Pobil** being particularly recommended for a little local atmosphere) (Wp.28 160M). To return to **Camp de Mar**, take **Calle Alemania** out of the square and cross over the main road to **Carrer Son Esteva** where there's a taxi rank (€5) and, just beyond the next major road, the central bus-stop.

For Port d'Andratx

We turn left at Wp.19 (75M) and simply follow the **Camí de sa Vinya** all the way to the **Cala Llamp** road (Wp.29 85M), where we turn right and descend to **Port d'Andratx** seafront (Wp.30 90M). The taxi rank is 100 metres to the left, the bus-stop 100 metres to the right.

Seen from the south, the headland on the northern flank of **Port d'Andratx** looks like a solid sweep of villas climbing to a crest that can only be a stone's throw short of **Sant Elm**. Happily, this is a deceptive impression and tucked between the two ports is a lovely little *cala* backed by a broad valley that, miraculously, has been abandoned by farmers without being snapped up by property developers.

In this itinerary we offer two options for exploring this semi-wilderness, a looped walk visiting the delightfully deserted **Cala d'Egos** or a linear route to **Sant Elm** using the descent of Walk 12 and returning to **Port d'Andratx** by the 16.15 Margarita ferry (€7 - see Walk 17).

** **Cala d'Egos** loop 2 hours 15 mins + 25M (return) if arriving on foot
linear to **Sant Elm** 2 hours 30 mins (including 800 metres on foot from the **Port d'Andratx** bus-stop)

* in **Port d'Andratx**

Access: on foot from **Port d'Andratx**.

To reach the start (by car or on foot) take **Carretera Aldea Blanca**, which starts seventy-five metres west of the **Port d'Andratx** marina bus-stop. Turn left 150 metres later on **Carrer de Cala d'Egos**, passing an *ayuntamiento* mapboard for **Pas Vermell**.

Fork right at a junction to stay on the **Carrer de Cala d'Egos**, which soon becomes a dirt track. Continue on the dirt track for a further 200 metres till it swings left and forks west/south-west (Wp.1 0M), at which point motorists should park alongside the track.

Immediately before the fork, a broad cairn-marked trail climbs to the north-west, rapidly crossing two bends in the main track (Wps.2,3 & 4). After climbing steadily through peaceful woodland, we approach the embankment of the track again (Wp.5 15M), this time bearing right without crossing the track then immediately forking left on a narrow path.

The path climbs behind a bend in the track then meanders alongside an undulating dirt causeway, which it eventually crosses, joining the track for the third time (Wp.6) beside a tall concrete reservoir. Thirty metres to the right, we take a final shortcut path joining a broader trail climbing from the left - this trail starts in front of the reservoir but is less clear from below. Bearing right, we climb to a junction of tracks next to unusual, twin lime-kilns on the **Coll des Vent** (Wp.7 25M).

We maintain direction (NW) on the central track as it climbs behind the **Urbanización Mont Port**, bringing into view the **Llebeig** lighthouse on the southern tip of **Dragonera** and the long ridge descending from **Es Tres Picons**.

Comellars de Can Rodella

The track curves around the deep bowl of the **Comellars de Can Rodella** and **Cala d'Egos**, occasionally dipping down to follow the lie of the land, but generally climbing gently.

At a junction with two tracks climbing from the **Urbanización Mont Port** (Wp.8 45M), we bear left. Ignoring a minor, overgrown branch to the right fifty metres later, we follow the main track as it curves round the low rise of **Puig d'en Ric** to a Y-junction with a broad, rough track descending steeply towards **Cala d'Egos** (Wp.9 55M), at which point our two options diverge.

For the linear route to Sant Elm

We bear right, climbing steadily behind the 313 metre summit, beyond which we have superb views of the **S'Arraco** valley and the high peaks of **S'Esclop** and **Galatzó**. The track then curves left, passing a branch to the telecommunications mast on **Es Tres Picons** (Wp.10), seventy-five metres after which, cairns mark the first of several slip-paths climbing to the **Pas Vermell** (Wp.13 of Walk 12). On the far side of the ridge, the path bears right, back towards the mast, then curves left below low crags and descends to a dirt track beside a green firefighting reservoir, where we join Walk 12 one hundred metres after Wp.12

For the loop to Cala d'Egos

We bear left at Wp.9. After a skittery descent on a loose surface, the track levels off amid pine trees, beyond which we come to a junction (Wp.11 60M).

The branch on the left leads to a *caseta* and terraces which were visible earlier on as we curved round the rim of the *comellars*.

Cala d'Egos

We carry straight on (SW), gradually bearing south before joining the main track descending from **Coll des Vent** (Wp.12 70M). Turning right, we now simply follow this track along a wild, winding torrent until it peters out behind the beach (Wp.13 90M).

Like nearly all the island's inaccessible coves, **Cala d'Egos** isn't exactly pristine, but in this instance there's not enough jetsam to spoil the pleasure of being here.

From the perspective of the beach, the very notion of slogging back up the main track to **Coll des Vent** is a deeply unappetizing prospect. Fortunately, there is an alternative and considerably more interesting route to take the edge off this climb.

Shortly before the track ends, a cairn marks a narrow path that runs along its southern side for five metres before passing under a windswept pine and veering right. The path climbs steeply for 100 metres then levels off briefly before climbing steadily to the end of a rough dirt track (Wp.14 100M). We follow this track towards the cliffs of **Puig des Migdia**, below which it veers sharp left for a long, gentle climb (NE) to a Y-junction (Wp.15 115M). Bearing right (contrary to what the cairn suggests), we climb more steadily for five minutes, rejoining the main track fifty metres from **Coll des Vent** (Wp.16).

From here, we can either follow the shortcut path used on the outward leg or, for a more gentle descent, stay on the main track as it winds through a series of long traverses.

This attractive tour through the countryside behind **Sant Elm** is ideal for a preliminary exploration of the area, getting your bearings and enjoying for the first time the superb, pretty well ubiquitous views of **Dragonera**. The diversion up to **Pas Vermell** and the triple summits of **Es Tres Picons**, is strongly recommended, views that are good from below becoming really great from above. The walk is generally easy and for the most part follows good dirt tracks and broad trails, but earns a relatively high exertion rate for a couple of steep climbs. The more complicated southern section of the loop has plenty of cairns and waymarks to facilitate pathfinding. I don't recommend trying it in reverse until you're familiar with the way down to **Cala es Conills** as the new flats behind the *cala* conceal the start of the path.

*in **Sant Elm**

Access: on foot from **Sant Elm**.

Starting from the **Plaza de Mossén Sebastia Grau** (Wp.1 0M) bus terminus next to the **Bar Es Molí** at the northern end of **Sant Elm**, we take **Avinguda de la Trapa**, carrying straight on at the junction with **Carrer Eolo** on a tarmac lane that runs into the **Camí de Can Tomevi** dirt track (Wp.2 5M). Ignoring a branch to the right, we follow this dirt track to a junction next to the deserted **Can Tomevi**, house Nº14, also distinguished by a mural including a rather discombobulated looking bull (Wp.3 15M). Ignoring tracks and trails to the left and directly ahead, we turn right, effectively staying on the same track, which is now called **Camí de Punta de Sa Galera**.

After passing two tracks branching left, the second leading to a house with a pebble-dash porch, we come to a major Y-junction (Wp.4 20M). The cairn-marked track to the left is the route followed in Walk 18, but for today's itinerary, we take the right-hand fork, staying on the main track. We soon see **Puig d'en Farineta** (see Walk 13) off to our right and can just make out the smooth line of the *mirador* on top. At a crossroads (Wp.5 25M), we turn right on **Camí sa Font dels Morers**, also signposted 'S'Arraco'. We now follow this track all the way to the PM103. Crossing a small rise, we come into view of the **Tres Picons** ridge, topped by a telecommunications mast. At the branch with the **Camí de Can Bolei** (Wp.6 40M), we continue on the **Camí sa Font dels Morers**, climbing to the parking area just west of **Coll de sa Palomera** (Wp.7 55M).

Twenty metres from the eastern end of the car-park, just past the rise of the *coll*, we cross the road onto a broad path climbing to a ruin, behind which are two abandoned terraces. We follow a very faint path across the lower terrace, passing several carob trees. We then descend onto another terrace (Wp.8 60M), after which a narrow but clear path descends to join a very narrow track (Wp.9 62M), known as **Barrí Son Tío**. N.B. The preceding 250 metres between the road and **Barrí Son Tío** crosses private property; it's abandoned

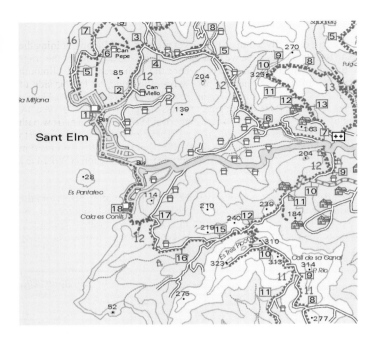

and unfenced, but that doesn't mean it won't be closed off in future. If it is, stay on the road for another fifty metres and, at a sharp left hand bend just above **S'Arraco** cemetery, you'll find the signposted start of the **Barrí Son Tío** track, which joins the direct route 75 metres after a small ruin. In either case, we follow the **Barrí Son Tío** track as it curves south-west to a Y-junction, where we bear left, descending to a bend in a narrow tarmac lane (Wp.10 65M).

Dragonera, as seen on the descent

Turning right, we follow this lane as it climbs steeply to the south-west. After levelling out briefly, the lane climbs a little less steeply and, thirty metres before it ends at the gates of a new house, we bear left at a Y-junction with a dirt track above an abandoned cabin (Wp.11 75M). Climbing along the track towards the **Es Tres Picons** ridge, we ignore a trail on the left just below a first short stretch of concrete. A little over five minutes later, **Dragonera** comes into view, after which we climb more steeply, passing two more stretches of concrete before coming to a cairn-marked path on the left, immediately before two charred gateposts (Wp.12 90M).

This is the start of the diversion up to **Pas Vermell/Es Tres Picons**. Joining the main path twenty metres later, we bear left, climbing steadily toward the crags below the telecommunications mast, where the path veers west, climbing along reddish rocks to the narrow pass across the ridge, on the far side of which is the valley behind **Cala d'Egos** (see Walk 11) (Wp.13 100M). Unless you want to go to **Port d'Andratx**, there's no great purpose served by descending on the far side, but on the northern side of the pass, a narrow path runs along the ridge for fifty metres to a superb natural *mirador*. We return to the main track by the same path (Wp.14). 25M (return) has been allowed in subsequent timings for this diversion. Otherwise, the Y-junction at Wp.14 is a little over five minutes from Wp.12.

Back on the dirt track, we continue past the green fire-fighting reservoir and, after taking advantage of a shortcut across a bend in the track, descend to a Y-junction (Wp.15 115M), where we fork right on a minor branch. This track, barely more than a broad trail, descends gently through a pleasant valley lightly wooded with young pine and wild olive.

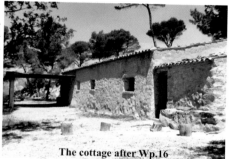

After another shortcut path, we join a better stabilized track for five metres then turn right (Wp.16 125M) to continue on a broad trail/narrow track, passing an attractive little woodland cottage and a sign prohibiting vehicles, after which we can see **Sant Elm**.

The cottage after Wp.16

After passing a chain, the track broadens and swings inland (NE) (Wp.17 140M), at which point, we turn left on a broad path marked with red and blue waymarks. The path runs along the southern side of a shallow gully to a Y-junction. Forking right, we follow the cairn-marked route descending to the left of and then in front of a small block of flats, below which we clamber onto the broad flight of steps behind the tiny harbour of **Cala es Conills** (Wp.18 150M). We now simply follow the road back to **Sant Elm**. For those who arrived by bus, the walk ends at the stop behind **Sant Elm** beach. Motorists should continue along the main pedestrian thoroughfare through **Sant Elm**. When it comes to an end, maintain direction for forty metres to **Plaza de na Caragola** then turn left on **Carrer Cala en Basset**, which leads back to the start of the walk.

In the rush to reach **Sa Trapa**, many of the shorter walks between **Andratx** and **Sant Elm** tend to be neglected or sketched in as part of a longer itinerary, which is a pity as this complex landscape deserves a more detailed exploration.

In this short but strenuous itinerary, we climb to **Puig d'en Farineta** (also known as **Puig d'en Basset**) a superb *mirador* above dramatic cliffs with commanding views of **Dragonera** and the major summits surrounding **Sant Elm**.

*in **S'Arraco**

Access: on foot from **S'Arraco**

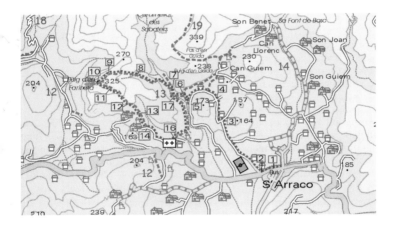

Starting from the **Plaza Toledo** bus-stop in **S'Arraco** (Wp.1 0M), we follow the **Sant Elm** road for 100 metres, then turn right on the **Camí des Castellas** (Wp.2). The tarmac lane ends at the local sports ground, and the **Camí des Castellas** continues as dirt track, climbing gently through scattered housing to a Y-junction, signposted 'Camí des Castellas 15 a 31' (Wp.3 15M), where we fork left, passing house N°38.

Five minutes later, at a crossroads in front of the entrance to house N°17 (Wp.4), we continue straight ahead on a broad trail, which gradually bears west, passing a tastefully restored house (N°101) with a large sun dial set into the wall. The trail then curves southwest, descending alongside a shallow, terraced valley, where we turn sharp right at a major junction with a broad path doubling back to the north (Wp.5 25M), crossing the terraced valley and passing the rock-like stump of a dead olive tree.

On the far side of the valley, we turn left on a path marked with cairns and a red arrow (Wp.6). The path curves into what initially appears to be an affluent of

The Torrent de Ca na Rosa valley

the shallow, terraced valley, but which, on rounding a bend, reveals itself to be the principal valley, the **Torrent de Ca na Rosa**. Immediately after the **Ca na Rosa** opens up, we leave the main path, forking left on a cairn-marked way (Wp.7 30M), crossing the dry course of the *torrent* and climbing onto the valley's western flank.

After a steady climb (WNW) between shrubby young pine, broom, cistus and *pistacia lentiscus*, during which we cross the trunks of several pine felled by forest fires, we enter the westernmost watershed feeding the **Ca na Rosa**, where we pass a large cairn amid a stand of surviving pine (Wp.8 40M). Seventy-five metres later, the path crosses the watershed and begins its steep climb up **Puig d'en Farineta**.

The way, which isn't always obvious from below but is clearly marked by cairns, winds between rock and palmetto, then veers left (WSW) below a small outcrop of rock topped with a pine. A final, virtually pathless but still clearly cairn-marked route then climbs to the left of the pine-topped rock, onto the sweeping blade of **Puig d'en Farineta** (Wp.9 55M) - the drop on the far side is particularly fierce here, so take care as you approach.

Bearing left and remaining a prudent five to ten metres from the edge, we follow a cairn-marked way along the escarpment to the west, descending slightly to the top of abandoned terraces. At the top of the terraces, we pick up a path climbing via a three-sided concrete hut (visible from Wp.6), to the *mirador* on the summit, where there's a ceramic plaque placed by the Grup Excursionista Badia Gran (Wp.10 70M). The views are extraordinary.

To descend, we follow a pathless, cairn-marked route along the rocky ridge to the southeast and, after fifty metres, pick up a faint, waymarked goat path.

The waymarks are generally placed for people climbing and the path is very faint, so keep an eye out for the cairns as you approach a slight dip in the ridge (Wp.11 75M), where the path, still rough but now much clearer, descends the western flank of the ridge towards a large new villa.

Descending the western flank of Puig d'en Farineta

Near the end of the ridge, **S'Arraco** comes back into view and we descend to a small stand of pine, where a maze of goat paths do the goatish thing and splinter off in all directions (Wp.12 90M). Following the cairn and waymarked route, we cross the stand of pine, 10 metres below which, the path swings left (E) away from the new villa, descending gently between a mixture of dead and dying pine to a T-junction with a path alongside a fence (Wp.13 95M).

Turning left, we follow the fence path, passing a large stone cabin, just below which we join a partially asphalted track (Wp.14). Bearing left, we follow this track down to the cemetery, behind which we again turn left on a dirt track (Wp.15 105M) running parallel to the **S'Arraco-Sant Elm** road. Behind a small house backed by an immense solar panel and satellite dish (Wp.16), we fork left on a narrow path descending to cross a small wood of pine, wild olive and oak. The path then climbs toward a tiny stone cabin, behind which it swings north alongside the southern end of the **Torrent de Ca na Rosa**. Descending into the valley, we meander through encroaching cistus, broom, *carritx*, *pistacia lentiscus*, honeysuckle and gladioli, passing to the left of a medium sized pine. After traversing a field of moribund almond trees, we cross the dry torrent and rejoin our outward route (Wp.17) one hundred metres from Wp.6 (120M).

The **Andratx** *ayuntamiento* route, 'Penya des Corb i Ses Rotes de s'Hereu', is a short loop with half a longer walk tacked onto the end of it to make it look more substantial! We cover the tacked on bit in Walk 19, but the short loop through the **Es Castellessets** area is a sufficiently attractive, leisurely country stroll to be worth describing as a discrete itinerary. If you don't fancy the strenuous circuit of Walk 19, the tacked-on-bit leads to several good picnic spots on the **Comellar des Sabaters** terraces and is nice enough to be walked both ways.

Access: on foot from **S'Arraco**

*in **S'Arraco**

Starting from the **Plaza Toledo** bus-stop below the clock tower in **S'Arraco** (Wp.1 0M), we walk up the main road toward **Andratx** for one hundred metres, passing the **Es Puput** restaurant, then turn left on **Calle del Porvenir**, forking right after another 100 metres at the junction with **Barrí Can Massana** (Wp.2). The **Calle del Porvenir** soon leads out of the village and comes to a fork of dirt tracks, signposted **Barrí Sa Clota** to the left (Wp.3 15M). We take the right hand fork, then bear left one hundred metres later on the **Barrí son Guiem** (Wp.4), another tarmac lane.

The lane runs between groves of almond, olive and carob, interspersed with the occasional pine or oak, then curves sharp left in front of **Sa Font des Bosc** (Wp.5 30M) and becomes a dirt track, climbing past **Can Llorenç** and **Son Benet**.

Restored house N°20

At a crossroads behind **Son Benet**, we turn left, then fork left again at the next Y-junction, after which the dirt track dwindles to a narrow path passing in front of twin restored houses (N°s 19 & 20).

Passing almond terraces dotted with poppies and mauve thistles, the path comes to a Y-junction on a mini-coll, the **Collet de Dalt** (Wp.6). Forking right, we climb behind a ruin (No.21) and the path broadens to a trail shortly before a major Y-junction (Wp.7 45M), which is where we join Walk 19 and have the option of taking the *ayuntamiento*'s 'tacked-on-bit'.

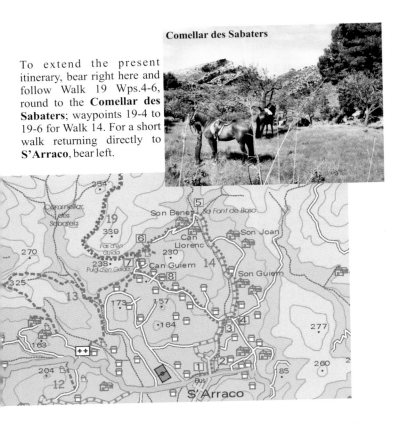

Comellar des Sabaters

To extend the present itinerary, bear right here and follow Walk 19 Wps.4-6, round to the **Comellar des Sabaters**; waypoints 19-4 to 19-6 for Walk 14. For a short walk returning directly to **S'Arraco**, bear left.

The trail on the left descends past **Can Corso**, broadening to a rough dirt track before joining a better stabilized track leading to a house with blue shutters. We bear right here and, after passing a waymarked path branching off to the right, carry straight on at a crossroads of dirt tracks below **Can Guiem** (Wp.8 55M). We are now on the **Barrí sa Clota** track, which we follow back to Wp.3, bearing right shortly after House N°13 and passing a house called **Casita de Perro** - The Kennel! From Wp.3 we return to **S'Arraco** by the same lane.

Garrafa is the Great Wall of the West, a cliff bound ridge dividing **Andratx** from **Calvià** and linking the high limestone mountains of the north to the low wooded hills of the south. Apart from the hum of traffic from the C719 that accompanies us throughout the climb, it's a wonderfully isolated and peaceful spot with superb views in every direction and was once a relatively easy walk. Sadly, the old route to the top via the **Coma de sa Teva** or **Teia** has been closed. Locals, notably climbers heading for the cliffs, still cheerfully clamber over the locked gates, but in keeping with our no-controversy rule, we follow a new route trail-blazed by more law-abiding but no less determined Mallorcan ramblers. This, however, is a very tough, pathless climb across sharp limestone clints and, though frequent cairns mean pathfinding is not a problem, it can only be recommended to experienced walkers accustomed to hopping about on ankle-twisting terrain.

GPS users will welcome waypoints 6 to 18 guiding them along the climb and ridge, where setting a proximity alarm for these waypoints will give an audible reminder of progress without having to look at the screen.

Other books that describe this walk tell you to walk along the road between **Andratx** and **Coll Andritxol**. This is insane. The C719 is not a road you want to stand on for more than a few seconds unless you fancy a flat head. I have seen one woman successfully negotiate it with a shopping trolley, but if you don't intend taking your shopping trolley with you (not recommended), there's no good reason for following the road, given that there's a perfectly serviceable track running alongside it.

If the route I describe to the coll happens to be fenced off in the future, do not walk along the road. Get a taxi to the **Depositos de Agua en Coll Andritxol**. The driver may grumble (it's a tricky turn-off and you'll probably have to go via **Camp de Mar** as the turning can only be taken from the east), but better a disgruntled driver than a biscuit-slim rambler.

** in view of the terrain, allow 4½ hours plus
* in **Andratx**

Access: on foot from **Andratx**

To reach the start by car, arriving in **Andratx** from **Camp de Mar**, turn right on **Carrer de Son Prim**, more obviously signposted 'Sa Coma'. Park 300 metres later at the junction with **Camí de Son Xina** and **Via Juan Riera**. To reach the start from the main bus-stop in **Andratx**, head away from the centre of town, crossing **Carrer des Carreters** and following **Carrer de Son Moner** as it curves to the left in front of **Colegio Ramon Llull**, then descend across the bridge to the junction of roads.

From the triple junction below **Son Xina** (Wp.1 0M), we follow **Carrer de**

Son Prim (motorists walking back the way they arrived) past a secondary school and **Andratx** sports centre to the **Palma** road (Wp.2), where we turn left. Follow the road uphill past the petrol station and **Eroski** supermarket then, when the pavement ends at the city limits (Wp.3 10M), dump your shopping trolley and take the rough dirt track to the left of the crash barriers. Just above the tunnel of the slip-road for **Port Andratx**, we ignore the overgrown trail climbing to the left, and maintain a southerly direction on a broad track along an almond and carob terrace thirty metres east of the road.

At the top of the **Port Andratx** slip-road, the track dwindles to a path, which we follow past new concrete posts carrying heavy-duty cables, passing above the **Coll Andritxol** junction of the new C719 and a long bend of the old road. The path continues alongside the old road, climbing slightly to pass an older wooden post carrying the same heavy-duty cable. Crossing a small rise, we see three large water reservoirs (the *depositos de agua*) and the gates blocking the **Sa Teva** dirt track. At the second wooden post, just before new fencing round the reservoirs, we step over a broken down fence (Wp.4 25M) and descend to the old road.

The **Coma de Sa Teva** route follows the track behind the locked gates on our left, but we continue along the old road as it curves round to closed metal gates, where we fork left on a narrow dirt track (Wp.5). One hundred metres along the track, at the cusp of a small rise, we turn left on a narrow path marked by cairns (Wp.6 30M). The path climbs steeply then steadily through the pines (N), detouring round the occasional fallen tree.

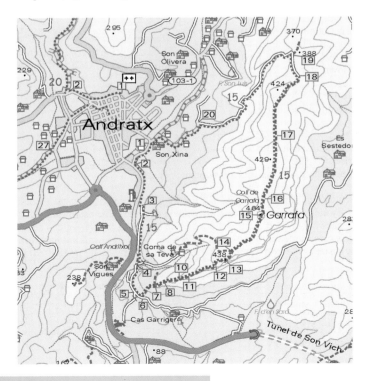

The ongoing route is frequently unclear from below, but in each instance reveals itself as you continue climbing. Just below the crest of a long sloping shoulder, the path bears right (E) crossing a small clearing before climbing again to a junction of cairn-marked paths (Wp.7 40M). Ignoring the path coming in from the left, we maintain our easterly direction, and the lavish care of local ramblers reveals itself in a flurry of cairns every few metres.

When the path bears left and appears to descend across the top of the shoulder (Wp.8 44M), we turn right, as indicated by a myriad of cairns, climbing across bare rock dotted with palmetto to duck under the single remaining strand of an old wire fence (Wp.9 45M).

Once past the fence, the long, hard slog up the pathless southern ridge of **Garrafa** begins. If you don't like the look of it from here, turn back now, because there's more of the same for a long time. For the next hour, it's essentially a question of following the cairns as there are few distinct physical features for making description meaningful. Likewise timings, which are always subjective, become almost meaningless on terrain like this. After Wp.10, stay well back from the cliffs on the right which, on such rough ground, constitute an even graver risk than usual.

All that said, don't be discouraged! There's pleasures as well as perils up here and you should stop once in a while, partly to recover your breath, but also so you can forget about the vertical tennis match of looking down at your feet, up at the next cairn, down at your feet, up, down, up, down … and enjoy the superb views that gradually unfold behind you.

Views west on the climb

After twenty minutes of uninterrupted climbing (it probably won't be uninterrupted so calculate accordingly), we cross the first of a succession of small rises (Wp.10 65M), bringing into view **Santa Ponça** and the **Túnel de Son Vich** to the south-east and **S'Esclop** to the north.

The broad slope of rock we've been climbing so far, now narrows to a ridge about fifty metres wide. Approaching the next rise, the ridge narrows further, and we pass a v-shaped cleft in the rocks on the right, where we can see a climber's cleat nailed into the clifftop (Wp.11 75M). The walking becomes slightly easier as the cairns guide us along a natural 'way' cushioned by sparse grass.

The 'way' is intermittent, broken up by sections of bare rock as we come to a third, slightly smoother rise on which there are two cairn-marked ways (Wp.12 95M). We opt for the slightly easier route on the left, away from the cliff edge. The two routes soon converge at a large, flattish pile of stones on the 438-metre top (Wp.13 105M). Relax! The worst is over.

We now follow the cairns across the plateau, passing a larger cairn on the left after 100 metres where we join the **Sa Teva** ascent (Wp.14), after which a faint path gradually emerges and the firewatch tower on the main summit comes into view.

The trig point at 120 minutes

Descending to a broad coll, we pick up old red and yellow waymarks, then climb across more rubble and rough rocks to the firewatch tower and trig-point (Wp.15 120M). The views are stupendous.

Twenty metres north-east of the firewatch tower, a narrow, rough, but clear path descends to the **Coll de Garrafa** (Wp.16 125M) where there's a large cairn and, on the left, an uprooted tree with a yellow waymark on its trunk, indicating another old path descending to very large and very locked gates in front of the petrol station. Continuing in a northerly direction, we climb across two small rises, the second very shallow. The path, which is pleasantly shady at this stage, runs along the eastern side of the ridge, then descends to a long, wooded coll, where it becomes slightly more obscure.

At an apparent Y-junction midway along the coll (Wp.17 140M), we follow the cairn-marked route to the right, which leads into more open, less densely forested land. The path then skirts to the right of a low, virtually treeless rise, passing a pothole, after which it curves round to the left and goes through a gap in a wall before descending to a grassy coll where the fire-wardens park their cars (Wp.18 155M).

Bearing left on a rough dirt track, we descend past a small cabin, immediately after which we ignore a trail continuing to the north (Wp.19) and follow the main track to the left. We now simply follow this track, ignoring all branches, as it winds down the mountain-side, a delightfully easy stroll that makes for a striking contrast with the strenuous climb across the rocks at the southern end of the ridge. When the track joins the end of a tarmac lane (Wp.20 185M), a branch of the **Camí de Son Simo**, we turn left and follow the lane back to the start of the walk.

Prejudices are never pretty, but for anyone used to walking in wild places, it's nearly always an occasion for rejoicing when a property developer goes bankrupt, and the gratification was almost palpable when the company 'developing'(as if anything so perfect actually required developing) the coast north of **Sant Elm**, got its sums wrong and went out of business. The debris they left behind has recently been cleared and some industrious dog-walking by local residents has resulted in a complex network of interlinking paths that will reward further exploration by anyone staying in **Sant Elm**. In this itinerary, we cross the defunct *urbanización* to visit the **Torre de Cala en Basset** watchtower and the creek after which it is named, then return via the **Camí de Can Tomeví**.

Access: on foot from **Sant Elm**   *in **Sant Elm**

The walk starts from the **Plaza de Mossén Sebastia Grau** (Wp.1 0M) bus terminus next to the **Bar Es Molí** at the northern end of **Sant Elm**. Ignoring the signposted route along **Avinguda de la Trapa**, we head north on **Avinguda s'Algar**, also signposted 'Mirador Sant Elm'. When the road reaches a T-junction (Wp.2), we turn left, climbing past the **Punt Blanc Residence** before turning right on **Carrer na Popia** (Wp.3).

At a crossroads beside a large yellow house at the end of the urbanized area, we can either continue straight ahead on a dirt track lined with kerbstones until we see a hand-painted 'TORRE' sign nailed to a tree, or (as mapped) descend to the right for 30 metres then turn left on a broad dirt trail (Wp.4 10M).

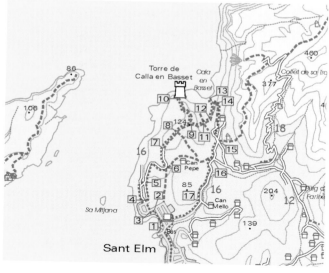

Forking left fifty metres later, we climb gently for 200 metres, then turn right on a branch track (Wp.5, the one with a hand-painted sign), almost immediately bearing left, as indicated by cairns and arrows of stones on the ground. The track climbs gently, curving NE/E/SE to a sharp left-hand bend (Wp.6), where it's joined by another path climbing from **Sant Elm**. We stay on the track as it continues climbing to the north and, fifty metres before it dwindles to an overgrown path, turn right on a broad cairn and waymarked path (Wp.7 25M).

This path, a positive gymkhana of fallen tree trunks, winds through the woods, passing a junction with a path on the right (Wp.8) before descending to a small clearing (Wp.9 35M) where paths branch left and right for the *torre* and the *cala*. Bearing left, we descend to the *torre* (Wp.10 40M), from where we have fine views of **Dragonera**, **Cala en Basset**, and the cliffs below **Sa Trapa**. After enjoying the views, we return to Wp.9 and take the other path descending to the east.

Cala en Basset

At a crossroads of paths (Wp.11), we carry straight on, continuing our descent to the flat bed of the valley (Wp.12 55M). Turning left on the nearside of the valley, we follow a pathless but clear route marked by cairns, descending across a succession of retaining walls to an improvised stone picnic table, after which we cross two more retaining walls to enter the boulder-strewn gully down to **Cala en Basset** (Wp.13 65M). The cove is a lovely, isolated spot, which you're likely to have to yourself apart from a few cormorants and the odd yacht; unfortunately the beach is bejewelled with jetsam and tends to trap the shoals of tiny blue jellyfish that are washed ashore in spring.

N.B. If there's a fishy sludge of decomposing jellyfish along the beach, don't dip your boots in it - the stink is all but ineradicable.

Retracing our steps to the stone 'table', we pick up a path climbing across the retaining walls on the eastern side of the valley to join a broad trail (Wp.14 70M). Turning right, we climb along the trail, which soon becomes a dirt track just below an attractive stone cottage. The track climbs to a locked gate, which we pass to the right, then swings left in front of a second gate before coming to two concrete gateposts and a crossroads of paths and tracks (Wp.15 75M), where we join the descent of Walk 18.

Turning right, we leave the dirt track and descend on a broad waymarked trail (SW) to join the **Camí de Can Tomeví** (Wp.16 80M). Maintaining direction (SW) and ignoring a fork on the left to **Can Melló** (Wp.17), we follow the main dirt track and the road it eventually runs into all the way back to our starting point, passing en route a house called **El Culo del Mundo**, a startlingly indelicate way of saying 'The Nether Ends of the World'.

The motto for this one is, "Don't just look at it, go there!" None of the classic walks near **Andratx** would be quite the same without their views of **Dragonera**, which must be one of the most photographed bits of rock in the western Mediterranean, yet relatively few ramblers actually visit the island itself. This is to be regretted as it's a delightful place, the pleasures of which are only intensified when you consider it came within a hair's breadth of being turned into an *urbanización,* a project that was only finally defeated in the late 1980s when, after years of popular protest, the *Consell de Mallorca* bought the island and instituted proceedings to turn it into a nature reserve.

The current *Parc Natural* is well-managed and a painstaking programme is underway, attempting to recreate the conditions required for biodiversity. Goats have been eliminated, so the flora is healthy and varied, but the fauna is still threatened by two predators (see the 'drawback' below and the note in the penultimate paragraph). In theory though, the island is a birdwatcher's paradise, boasting Eleanor's Falcons, Audouin Gulls (both rare, the latter only found in the Balearics and Eastern Mediterranean), Cory's Shearwater, Storm Petrel, and Shag.

June Parker (see Bibliography) describes an interesting off-path walk following the cliff-tops on the western side of the island. Unfortunately, since its incorporation as a natural park, off-path walking is no longer permitted and we are obliged to stick to the four approved itineraries: to the **Es Lladó Mirador** (thirty minutes); to the **Cap de Tramuntana** lighthouse (one hour); to the abandoned lighthouse, **Far Vell**, on **Na Pòpia** (also known as **Na Popi**), the island's summit (three hours); and to the Cap des Llebeig lighthouse (two hours forty minutes). The times in brackets are the official, return times.

The described itinerary climbs to the **Na Pòpia** lighthouse, though all routes are signposted and easy to follow. Despite its apparent inaccessibility from a distance, the walk up **Na Pòpia** is very easy. The path is beautifully graded, the climb gentle throughout, and there are no pathfinding difficulties.

There is, however, one drawback: come spring when they're nesting, the herring gulls don't like being disturbed by ramblers. In fact, they're absolutely bloody livid and spend their time dive-bombing you, squawking, yapping and yowling, and generally carrying on for all the world as if you're a fishing smack returning to port. So if you suddenly get the impression you've got a Yorkshire Terrier yelping at your neck, don't be surprised.

However, you should not be alarmed by this on two counts. First, these gulls are a pest driving out all competitors. They're so fierce, even the Peregrine Falcons are frightened of them, and the only rival they'll tolerate are the cliff-dwelling Eleanor Falcons. The park authorities are currently trying to reduce their numbers by going from nest to nest and spiking two in three eggs with a needle (you can imagine how popular _that_ is) and, when we asked about the gulls, we were airily told to simply 'wave a stick over your head' to keep them away! The second reason you needn't really worry (and why you don't absolutely have to look like a deranged tour guide who's lost his umbrella) is that the gulls rarely come closer than a couple of feet. The scene may resemble the Battle of Britain with squadrons of beady-eyed daredevils scrambling into action to defend the homeland, but they don't actually attack, and the worst they're liable to do is defecate on you - admittedly with remarkable accuracy, but that's all. That said, if you have an aversion to birds, stay at home.

Access: by boat from **Sant Elm** or **Port d'Andratx**.

The Margarita ferry leaves **Sant Elm** from the jetty below **Restaurante El Pescador** on **Avinguda Jaume I**. Scheduled departures are at 10.15, 11.15, 12.15, 13.15 & 14.45, the return about 15 minutes later, or as requested - you'll be asked when you want to come back on the outward journey. The fare, payable on the return leg, is €9. The same boat links **Port d'Andratx** and **Sant Elm** at 8.30 and 16.15 (€7).

From the mapboard above the **Cala Lladó** landing (Wp.1 0M), we walk past the small museum (worth visiting for details on the island's history, natural and otherwise) and turn left at the signposted junction (Wp.2) of the **Llebeig** and **Tramuntana** itineraries. Strolling along a narrow tarmac lane (S) we cross a small bridge Wp.3), then turn right on the signposted trail for 'Es Far Vell/Na Popi' (Wp.4 10M) - there's also a sign in four languages (not English!) warning that the **Far Vell** buildings and terrace are unsafe and should not be entered. We now simply follow this trail to the top.

The trail climbs past small olive trees then goes through a gateway into the terraced belt of the **Comellar des Coll Roig**.

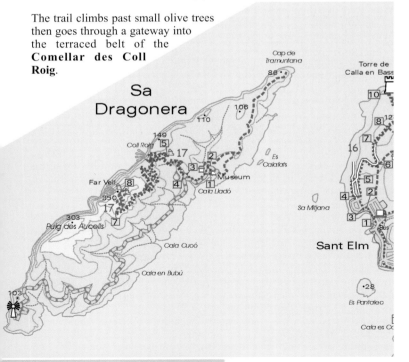

Tracing long zigzags back and forth across the shallow valley, we pass an attractive cabin (Wp.5 20M), gulls standing sentinel on every rock and thousands of greenish lizards (*sargantana*, the Balearic Lizard) rustling in the grass. Going through a second gateway (Wp.6 25M), we bear right and walk alongside a wall to **Coll Roig**, from where we get our first glimpse of the western cliffs - not too close a glimpse though, it's already a sheer 100 metre drop and this is not the place to be dancing about trying to dodge an angry seagull.

The trail now dwindles to a path, doubling back SE along the first of a succession of retaining walls, raised by prisoners when the lighthouse was built in the nineteenth century. The path climbs between banks of *pistacia lentiscus*, broom, euphorbia and wild olive, and superb views open out over the **Es Freu** straits. You may notice holed buckets along the path here. These are aimed at the island's other great predator, rats. The buckets contain an anticoagulant that causes haemorrhages in the menstruating rats killing them off. It's not very pretty, but in an enclosed environment where rats are virtually the only mammals apart from a few tiny hares, it's preferable to poison.

The path gets stonier the higher we go, zigzagging through increasingly tight switchbacks, after which a long, less rocky, southwesterly traverse brings the southern end of the island into view. Doubling back NNW (Wp.7 55M), we see, in gradual succession, **S'Esclop** behind **Sa Trapa**, the ruins of **Far Vell** above us, and the **Puig des Aucells** trig-point to the south.

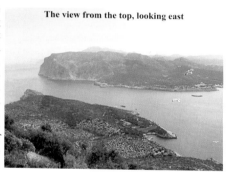

The view from the top, looking east

After a tiny refuge, we double back for the last time and pass below the **Far Vell** ruins (Wp.8 75M). The views from the end of the path are sensational. We return by the same route.

Trappist monks are generally known for their rule of silence and for brewing some of the best beers available on the continent, but they have also displayed what, at first glance, seems like an uncanny knack for locating their monasteries in the sort of perfect wild places that appeal to modern day ramblers. This is perhaps less surprising when you consider that both parties, albeit for slightly different reasons, seek solitude and an escape from the chatter and clatter of the urban world. The monastery at **Sa Trapa** was only occupied for fourteen years, but the brevity of the monks' stay should not lead you to conclude their eye for a landscape was in anyway impaired.

Tucked into an isolated valley above a plummeting drop into the Mediterranean and confronting the surging sea-monster of **Dragonera**, **Sa Trapa** is one of Mallorca's great sites and should be a place of pilgrimage no matter what manner of god you worship. This, the shortest and simplest of our three itineraries visiting the monastery, is a variant on the classic linear route popular with walkers and tourists staying in **Sant Elm**.

** 2 hours 20 min - 3 hours
* in **Sant Elm**

Access: on foot from **Sant Elm**

We start as per Walk 12 (Wps.1-4), but leave the **Camí de Punta de Sa Galera** after the house with a pebble-dash porch, forking left on a broad track marked with a cairn (Wp.5 20M). Ignoring a first branch on the right (NE), we

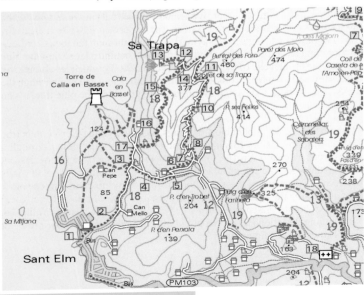

stick to the main track (NW), which climbs steadily then levels off as it approaches a second junction, this time with a narrow woodland path (Wp.6 25M). We follow this path (E) for a couple of minutes until it runs into a bend on another dirt track (the **Camí Coll des Cairats**), at which point we turn left (Wp.7). We stay on this track all the way to **Sa Trapa**, so if you don't care to pace progress, shut the book now.

Ignoring a branch track at the next U-bend (Wp.8), we climb through a series of switchbacks, passing a chain and a wooden signpost for the 'Reserva Natural La Trapa' (Wp.9 45M). The track continues climbing steadily past a series of small terraced fields and a tiny stone cabin (Wp.10 55M), after which the climb steepens for the final approach to the **Collet de sa Trapa** (also known as **Coll** or **Pas de ses Animes** or **Coll des Cairats**) (Wp.11 70M), from where we can see the monastery itself, a view so spectacular it suggests it wasn't just God and good Belgian beer that rendered the monks mute. Ignoring all branches, we now simply follow the track through a gentle descent down to the ruins (Wp.12 80M).

Dragonera as seen from the mirador

After visiting the ruins and the superb if somewhat vertiginous *mirador* (Wp.13 not counted in subsequent timings), we retrace our steps to the bend behind the main building and the start of our return path, signposted 'Sant Elm 1h' (Wp.14).

The path climbs gently (SE) for five minutes before curving round below the **Ses Animes** crags to the start of a steep, rocky descent down to a clear dirt path. For the easiest of various waymarked routes through the rocks, we keep bearing right until we traverse a shoulder of rock behind a large, solitary pine and join the rough head of the clear path (Wp.15 95M), which levels out fifty metres lower down. N.B. Looking back at it from below, the way through the rocks clearly doesn't exist, but as long as you go behind the pine tree, it's an easy descent.

The path follows a contour below the crags, passing a large fallen boulder (the scar of which is visible fifty metres above the path!) and going through a natural rock gateway (Wp.16 110M), after which we begin our steady descent through the woods between **Cala en Basset** and **Can Tomevi**. The path winds between rocks and trees, passing shortcuts that serve no great purpose other than distressing the knees, before coming to a junction of trails and tracks next to two concrete gateposts (Wp.17 125M), where we join Walk 16. Maintaining direction (SW) on a broad trail, we rejoin our outward route at **Can Tomevi** a few minutes later.

If you only have time for one approach to **Sa Trapa**, this is the one to take, crossing the wild country between **S'Arraco** and **Ses Basses**, and taking in the toe-curling *mirador* above **Cap Fabioler** en route to the monastery. Despite the comparatively complex lay of the land and one or two critical and slightly obscure junctions, pathfinding is reasonably straightforward. However, a multiplicity of possible endings makes the itinerary resemble one of those Sunday newspapers that keep dismantling themselves in a bid to win new readers, so all options should be considered carefully before setting out to see which best suits your circumstances.

Access: on foot from **S'Arraco**

*in **S'Arraco**

The walk starts from the **Plaza Toledo** bus-stop in **S'Arraco** and follows the same route as Walk 13 until the crossroads in front of the entrance to house N°17 (20M). As in Walk 13, we continue straight ahead at the crossroads, passing house N° 21. Fifty metres after house N°21, and within sight of the restored house with a sundial on the wall, we leave the **Puig d'en Farineta** trail, turning left on a narrow path partially obscured by a large carob tree (Wp.1 23M). Though obvious once you've seen it, this path is easily missed. If you find yourself passing the house with the sundial (N°101), turn back.

Defined by low walls and hedged by oleaster, the narrow path runs between fields, crossing a rough gate. Ignoring faint traces to the right immediately after the gate, we maintain direction (NE) to join a dirt track at a bend (Wp.2 30M), after which we briefly follow Walk 14 in reverse. Turning left on the dirt track, then left again when we see a house with blue shutters 100 metres to the east, we climb past **Can Corso**, after which the track dwindles to a trail that gradually levels off as it approaches a junction with another trail doubling back to the left (Wp.3 35M).

Turning left, we follow this trail as it climbs steadily along the southwestern flank of **Puig d'en Guida**, to a first mini-coll, the **Pas d'en Guida** (Wp.4 45M). A narrow path on the left climbs to a natural *mirador* on **Puig d'en Corso** while an even narrower path to the right appears to climb onto **Puig d'en Guida**. We continue straight ahead on the main trail, which runs on the level for a while before climbing through a chicane to a shallow cutting forming a second small coll (Wp.5 55M) from where we descend into the **Comellar des Sabaters**.

This broad valley, essentially a large swale leading into the **Torrent de Ca na Rosa**, is also known as the **Rotes de s'Hereu**, a *rota* being a mountain smallholding with a cabin. Certainly the *casetas*, mostly in ruins, are well in evidence as our trail climbs along the southern side of the valley. If you're doing this path as an extension of Walk 14, the grassy terraces behind the two roofed *casetas* halfway up the valley make for a pleasant picnic spot.

Otherwise, stay on the main trail as it dwindles to a path, climbing across rocky ground carpeted with *pistacia lentiscus*, cistus, *carritx*, and palmetto.

Ignoring a couple of minor branches off to the left, we climb to a major Y-junction (Wp.6 75M) below the **Caseta de l'Amo en Pep** and **Coll des Cucons**, from where we can see the distinctive peaks of **Puig des Campás** and **Puig des Tancat** to the east, and to their left the main summit of **S'Esclop**.

The two paths soon rejoin, but the branch passing the ruined *caseta* is slightly more obscure, so we fork right, climbing across the rise behind the ruin. After the two paths rejoin, we continue over the rise, bringing into view (NW) the small stand of trees round the **Casetas de ses Basses**.

The north coast seen from behind Ses Basses

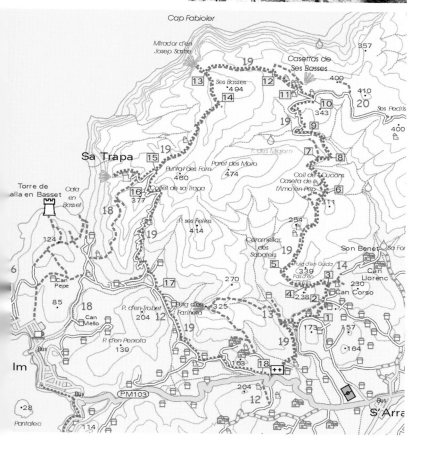

The path follows a contour above the valley of **Torrent Gore d'en Betts** (also known as **Torrent de sa Font**), gradually curving northeast and approaching a Y-junction (Wp.7 87M). Forking right, as indicated by cairns and faint waymarks, we descend toward the bed of the torrent. There are several interlinking routes here, but all rejoin on a clear path (Wp.8 90M) heading NW along a low retaining wall, eventually joining the end of a dirt track (Wp.9 100M) fifty metres behind a small flood dam. After a steady climb, the track levels out and, 200 metres later, joins the main track from **Sa Gramola** (Wp.10 115M), at which point we join Walk 20, turning left to climb to the **Casetas de ses Basses**.

We now follow Walk 20 (Wps.7-11, here numbered 11-14) to the west until it joins the dirt track behind the monastery (Wp.15 180M), at which point we have three distinct options:

First Option

If you only have time for one walk in the area and would rather not do anymore climbing, descend to the monastery then follow Walk 18 down to **Sant Elm**. For a brief description of the **Camí Can Tomevi** in this direction see Walk 16 Wp.16.

Second Option

If you only have time for one walk in the area and demand a loop to satisfy your sense of symmetry (or more simply just to get back to the car), descend to the monastery then follow Walk 18. Turn left at the concrete gateposts and follow the dirt track till it joins the **Camí Punta de sa Galera**. Turn left again to rejoin the option described below at Wp.17.

Third Option

If you've already explored or intend to make further explorations of the area and just want the most direct route back to **S'Arraco**, turn left on the dirt track and do the ascent of Walk 18 in reverse. This is the option described below.

Turning left on the dirt track, we climb for five minutes to the **Collet de sa Trapa** (Wp.16), from where we can see our descent coiling away below us. We now simply follow the track as it descends towards **Puig d'en Perxota**, passing a *caseta* (200M) and the cairn-marked trail branching west toward **Sant Elm** (220M), after which we continue on the main track to the junction with the **Camí Punta de sa Galera** and the **Camí sa Font des Morers** (Wp.17 225M).

Turning left, we follow the **Camí sa Font des Morers** all the way to **Coll de sa Palomera** on the PM103 (Wp.18 255M) (see Walk 12 for more detail). Bearing left on the road, we cross the coll then turn left again on a path cutting a bend in the road and descending to the **S'Arraco** cemetery, where we bear left yet again on the **Camí de son Veri**. Behind the cemetery, we turn right on a dirt track, picking up the end of Walk 13. If you haven't already done this path in full, we turn right after crossing the dry torrent, then right again fifty metres later, crossing a terrace on the left bank of the *torrent*. At a junction with a broad stony trail, we turn sharp left to return to Wp.1 of the present itinerary (280M).

This long, linear route follows a peaceful country lane and easy cart track up to **Coll de sa Gramola** to join the popular **Camí de ses Basses** track approaching **Sa Trapa** from the east. From the **Casetas de ses Basses**, we follow a stony trail across a wild and desolate landscape, visiting en route the most sickeningly spectacular *mirador* I ever hope to encounter. The descent to **Sant Elm** is the same as in Walk 18. If you're staying in **Sant Elm**, it's best to get an early start with the 8.30 a.m. bus to **Andratx**. If you're returning to **Andratx** at the end of the walk, buses leave **Sant Elm** at 2.15 p.m., 3 p.m., & 6 p.m..

** but in view of the length and the views, allow 6 hours
* in **Sant Elm**

Access: on foot from **Andratx**, returning by bus

Our itinerary starts one hundred metres west of **Andratx** church, in the **Plaza des Pau** (Wp.1 0M), on the PM103 to **S'Arraco** and **Sant Elm**. As the housing becomes less dense and we approach the edge of town, we turn right on **Carrer Barcelona** (Wp.2 10M), which soon becomes the **Camí de sa Coma Freda**. We now simply follow this pleasant country lane all the way to the head of the **Son Sampol** valley, climbing gently along the eastern flank of the valley and forking right at the junctions with the **Camí Son Avidal** (Wp.3 25M) and the **Camí des Torrent des Pont** (Wp.4 35M).

Seventy-five metres after passing a lane branching left down to properties N°s 39 & 41, the **Camí de sa Coma Freda** swings sharp right and we turn left on a cart track (Wp.5 50M) N.B. Ignore waymarking arrows on a wall to the right. The track briefly dwindles to a trail as it winds through the woods just below the main road, passing a cairn marked trail that descends to the left.

At a bend in a better stabilized track leading to a gated property on the left, we carry straight on and, ignoring a first branch up to the road, climb to the **Coll de sa Gramola** at km 106 of the C710 (Wp.6 65M). Turning left across the **Sa Gramola** parking area, we take the **Camí de ses Basses**, signposted 'Camí des Campás' and 'Ses Basses/La Trapa/Sant Elm'.

Sticking to the main track as it passes behind a small new house, we climb across a low rise where views open out of **S'Esclop** to the east and the **Coma de s'Evangèlica** to the north. The track climbs toward a high, bare, broken landscape of limestone patched with *carritx*, *pistacia lentiscus*, cistus and palmetto - not a place to be when it's hot, but otherwise a very impressive sweep of rock and scrub. After passing a major branch descending on the right to the **s'Evangèlica** farmhouses (Wp.7), the track tunnels through sickly pine then traverses meadows of wild grasses, thistles and asphodels, immediately

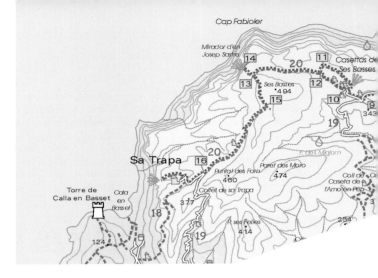

after which, we bear right at a Y-junction (Wp.8 80M).

We continue climbing, crossing the **Ses Pedrisses** heights, on the far side of which the track is cut to traffic by a chain, and we begin a long gentle descent, curving round the northern rim of the spectacular but bleak wilderness of the **Gore d'en Betts** valley. thirty metres after the walls of a tiny ruin, we fork right at a Y-junction (Wp.9 95M) and follow the track till it ends at the **Casetas de ses Basses** (Wp.10 100M), one tiny stone hut and two abandoned cabins - though only one is immediately visible.

From here, we can either follow the main trail in front of the first *caseta*, or take a narrower path behind it. If you choose the second option (recommended for the views) bear right at the *caseta*, then follow the clear but narrow path through the *carritx*.

At a large cairn (Wp.11), ignore a branch on the right (which disappears in the rocks) and bear left to rejoin the main route 350 metres from the first *caseta* (Wp.12 115M). We then continue in a westerly direction on the main trail, which soon dwindles to a stony path, climbing across two rocky rises onto a broad plateau below the **Ses Basses** trig-point.N.B. You can easily add fifteen minutes for simply standing still and staring at the views between Wps.10&13

At the western end of the plateau, a chest high cairn (Wp.13 130M) marks a branch to a small *mirador* one hundred metres to the north-west (Wp.14). N.B. Officially the **Mirador d'en Josep Sastre**, this spot is better known simply as **Cap Fabioler** after the cliffs below the *mirador* - immediately below it, 400 metres of them, straight down. The view of **Dragonera** is probably the most spectacular to be had from anywhere, but anyone who suffers from vertigo should stand well back. It's utterly horrible!

Somewhat less dramatically, we can also see from this point the fields behind **Sa Trapa** and the track descending from the **Collet de sa Trapa**. Returning to the chest-high cairn, we descend from the **Ses Basses** plateau on a well-trodden way weaving through the rocks in a generally southerly direction to a

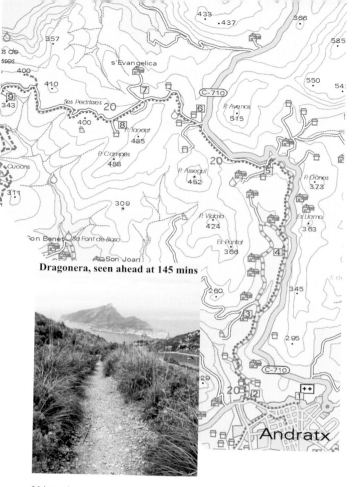

Dragonera, seen ahead at 145 mins

Y-junction just below the ridge (Wp.15 145M). Forking right, we head for the extraordinary silhouette of **Dragonera**.

Sa Trapa monastery

After descending gently, our path drops down to the fire-ravaged terraces behind **Sa Trapa**, passing fifty metres above two small ruins and crossing a wall before joining a bend in the dirt track (Wp.16 160M) a little way below the *collet*. Bearing right, we descend to the monastery. For the descent to **Sant Elm** see Walk 18 and Walk 16.

The westernmost summit of the **Tramuntana**, **S'Esclop**, is seen from many of the southern itineraries, looming over the **Calvià** plain like an immense cobbler's last, taking the **Es Moleto** pinnacle as the heel and the main summit as the sole. 'Esclop' means 'clog' in Catalán, doubtless an allusion to this curious shape, since anyone coming up here in clogs would be in serious difficulties.

Despite my airy assertions in the introduction that no special equipment was required for the walks in these books, this one should not be approached without proper gear: stout boots or tough walking sandals, appropriate clothing, picnic and plenty of water are all essential. Although it starts on the same track as our northern ascent of **Galatzó** (see Walk 22), it's much tougher as a large part of the route is pathless. Cairns are plentiful and pathfinding is not a major problem, but it's not an itinerary for the inexperienced. Given that cairns are often the only indication of where we're going, good visibility is essential.

It's worth pausing occasionally on the outward leg after Wp.5 to memorize the lay of the land for the return.

*   but allow at least 6 hours

Access: by car and (adding 2 kilometres return on the road) bus

We start from km 97 of the C710 on a good track (Wp.1 0M) (signposted 'Boal ses Serveres/Puig de Galatzó') climbing into the **Son Fortuny Àrea Recreativa**. There's space for parking immediately east of the track and, in the unlikely event that this is full, fifty metres up the track just before the chain against unauthorized traffic - though, as ever, take care not to block the entrance which may be used by firefighters and forestry workers. The nearest bus-stop is one kilometre to the west at the **Es Grau Restaurant**.

The track climbs steadily, superb views rapidly opening out over the coast, passing a branch on the right (Wp.2 15M) to the **Sa Coma** farm. We then descend slightly, coming into view of the **Pas de Cossis** between high cliffs on the left and lower crags on the right. After crossing a small rise and dipping down briefly, the track climbs steadily again, then veers left to a picnic area featuring a charcoal-burning circle and a roughly thatched re-creation of a charcoal burner's hut. Immediately before concrete gateposts (Wp.3 20M), we turn right for 'Pas de Cossis/Puig de Galatzó' following a broad trail climbing directly behind the hut. Climbing between bushy oak, the trail dwindles to a clear, rocky path, then zigzags up through a cascade of *carritx* to the **Pas de Cossis**, where there's a junction of paths and another 'Puig de Galatzó' signpost (Wp.4 35M).

Turning right (**S'Esclop** is not signposted but the name has been scratched

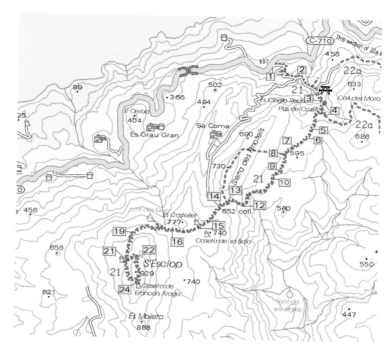

onto the back of the signpost), we cross an area of *carritx* covered scrubland dotted with newly planted pine, climbing toward the **Es Cingle Redó** cliffs. The path is relatively clear, but so are confusing patches of *carritx*-fringed ground, so follow the cairns, which gradually lead us (SSW) to a wide rock 'gateway' where roughly painted red waymarks indicate 'Galatzó' (SE) and 'Esclop' (SW) (Wp.5 45M) and we see the 'clog' for the first time.

This is where pathfinding becomes complex. Although we cross frequent stretches of something resembling a path, they never last long and the next forty-five minutes are essentially off-path. There are occasional waymarks - faded, covered in *carritx* and artfully painted the same hue as the lichen! Fortunately, there are dozens of cairns. These cairns are your best friends up here. There are two extra waypoints for those using GPS, but timings are given at greater intervals.

Maintaining a southerly direction through the gateway of rock, we follow the cairns, picking our way between limestone boulders and *carritx*. Checking each successive cairn then looking where you're putting your feet then checking the next cairn, you feel like a nodding dog on the back shelf of a car, but there's nothing else for it as the ground is rough and the cairns essential. After one hundred metres (Wp.6) we bear right, making for a tall cairn on a small rise (Wp.7 55M), after which the **Calvià** plain comes into view as we traverse a shallow swale. On the far side of the swale, a little over one hundred metres from Wp.7, cairn-marked routes divide beside two large, embattled pine (Wp.8).

The route to the west crosses the rise of the **Serra des Pinotells** before descending to the 652-metre *coll*. However it was never properly marked and is now badly overgrown at the end, so we fork left, following the main cairn-marked way, descending in a southerly direction toward a shallow, rocky valley spotted with palmetto (Wp.9 65M). As we descend into the valley, an affluent of the **Torrent de s'Esclop**, cairn-marked routes divide once again, but soon rejoin at a distinctively large cairn on a bare shelf in the middle of the valley (Wp.10 70M).

Climbing a small rise, we come into view of the two principal watersheds feeding the **Esclop** *torrent* and, at the head of the nearest watershed, a stretch of wall. We now follow a slightly clearer dirt path, deep in *carritx*, down to the nearest watershed, then climb to the eastern end of the wall (Wp.11 85M). After following the wall as it curves round the next rise, we veer right (Wp.12 90M) and start zigzagging up what is by local standards a clear path, passing a wall topped with barbed wire (Wp.13 where the old, direct route over the **Serra des Pinotells** descends to rejoin our route). Continuing alongside the wall, we come to the 652-metre *coll* (Wp.14 105M).

From the coll a grassy path dotted with daisies and asphodels climbs to the west. The path becomes rockier as it climbs and forks amid dense banks of *carritx*, but the two branches soon rejoin. There are actually several ways winding through the *carritx* here, but whichever one you find yourself on, simply maintain a westerly direction and you will soon come to a threshing circle (Wp.15 120M) identifiable from below by a retaining wall topped by a tall cairn. The diminutive summit to the north is variously called **Penya Blanca** or **Es Castellet**, while the ruin to the south is the **Caseta de sa Bala**. From the threshing circle, a gentle stroll on a clear path leads to the **Coll d'es Quer**, just below **S'Esclop** (Wp.16 125M).

Font d'es Quer

The main path crosses the *coll* to climb directly to the top. For a roundabout but more attractive and slightly easier ascent, we turn right, descending fifty metres to a narrow but clear path leading to the **Font d'es Quer**, a meagre spring tucked behind three tall poplars.

Fifty metres before the spring, just before the path passes between the first large outcrop of rock on the right and a large boulder on the left (Wp.17 130M), we climb to the left of the large boulder. At first, the 'way' is narrow, steep and obscure, but after about fifty metres it levels off and becomes slightly clearer (Wp.18 135M). If in doubt, keep on climbing, keeping the boulder spill to your left and the outcrops of rock behind the spring to your right, until you see a small, solitary pine.

Passing to the left of the solitary pine, we see a second solitary pine about one hundred metres further west and up to our left. Thirty metres after passing below this second pine, we bear left (Wp.19 140M), following a faint, cairn-marked way climbing steadily (SSE). The path becomes obscure again next to a large upright boulder (Wp.20 150M), but maintaining direction (SE), we soon come to another threshing circle and a ruin (Wp.21 155M), from where we can see **Port d'Andratx**.

Directly behind the threshing circle are low crags and, to their left, you will see two distinct declivities in the summit. Climbing to the left of the crags, we pick up a faint sheep's path heading NE to the most northerly of the two declivities, where cairns mark a simple traverse doubling back (ESE) to the head of the southernmost declivity (Wp.22 165M).

On top at 175 minutes, the trig point just visible

Bearing right, we cross rough rocky ground behind the crags then, when the southern coast comes back into view after seventy-five metres, scramble across large boulders to the left before bearing right (WSW) to the trig-point (Wp.23 175M).

The ruin seventy-five metres to the south is the hut where the French scientist François Arago lived while taking triangulation measurements in the early nineteenth century.

We return the same way, except for the initial descent. Midway between **Aroyo's hut** (Wp.24) and the trig-point, there is a clear, cairn-marked descent that's an easier way down but difficult to find from below. It emerges one hundred metres south of the threshing circle (Wp.25). Do not try to find the direct route back to **Coll d'es Quer**, which is difficult to locate even if you've just climbed it. Take particular care to follow the cairns-marked way down between Wps.14 & 12 as it's easy to stray too far east too early and get lost in the *carritx*.

The mountain that needs no introduction: you'll have been watching it from just about every other walk in the book and will know that, though far from being the highest summit on the island, it is one of Mallorca's most distinctive peaks. We offer two approaches, both ending with the same easy scramble to the top.

Both routes are relatively straightforward, even the longer of the two following good, waymarked tracks and paths, but neither should be underestimated. In particular, don't be deceived by the diminutive squiggle representing Version (b) on the map, still less by the apparent stone's-throw proximity of the summit when you reach the starting point. It may be the 'easy' way up, but it's still a rigorous climb on rough terrain and should not be undertaken casually. That said, provided you come prepared, either itinerary is a good way of getting a feel for high places and deciding whether mountain-tops are your thing. Those who already know will not be disappointed.

(a) Estellencs: Galatzó from the North

5 | 3¾-4H | 11 km | 800m / 800m | 0

Access: by car and (adding 2 kilometres return on the road) bus

This version starts as per Walk 21 (Wps.A1-A4), climbing through the **Son Fortuny Àrea Recreativa** to the **Pas des Cossis** (Wp.A4 35M). Turning left for **Puig de Galatzó**, we traverse the fire-ravaged terrain of **Es Pinotells**, passing a well and the first of numerous *sitjes* attesting to the former abundance of trees.

We then climb steadily (N) before emerging on the **Coll des Moro** (Wp.A5 50M), from where we can see **Galatzó**.

Looking towards Estellencs on route (a)

We now have a relaxing stroll (S then E) on a good path marked with cairns and wayposts. After crossing twin *sitjes*, we follow a slightly narrower path winding up a shallow, rocky watercourse, passing an unmarked branch to the right and bringing **Estellencs** into view.

A final steady climb leads through a natural rock gateway to a junction of paths at the **Pas de na Sabatera** (Wp.A6 80M) where there is welcome shelter in the shape of an overhanging rock shielding a rough plank bench.

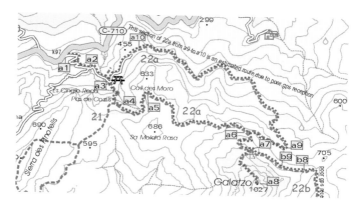

Turning right, we climb steeply on a well-trodden way marked with cairns. The gradient eases slightly as we bear right (W), skirting a first outcrop of rock, then left alongside a second outcrop (SE then E), leading to the junction with Version (b) at a signpost and the foundations of a small hut (Wp.A7 90M). Turning right (SW), we climb a rough, stony path behind the foundations of the hut then, after following a clear stretch of path for seventy-five metres, bear left up the splintered course of a watershed.

At the top of the watershed, we continue climbing steadily, maintaining direction (S) and heading for three vertical blue stripes on the rocks ahead. On closer inspection, the blue 'stripes' reveal themselves to be a cheery 'Hi', next to which an arrow and the word 'Principio' carved into the rock indicate the final, easy fifty-metre scramble to the trig-point on the summit (Wp.A8 120M).

On the summit, a plaque praises harmony and the sanctity of life, suggesting that 'once we have discovered ourselves, we have discovered God', and three mirrors give us the opportunity to gaze upon our own glassy divinity. Otherwise the views are great. Looking back the way we've come, we can see the trail we took from **Coll des Moro** and beyond it the curve of the **Es Moro** clifftop, below which lies our return route. We descend via the same route, taking care on the unstable stones, to **Pas de na Sabatera** (Wp.A6 150M).

At the **Pas de na Sabatera**, we bear right for **Font de Dalt**, going through a second natural rock gateway to join a good clear path descending (ESE) to the mixed woodland on the slopes behind **Estellencs**.

(Note that we had poor GPS reception after Wp.A6 but have left Wp.A9 in as possibly receivable, but we do not get good reception until we reach Wp.A10.)

Passing a sign for 'Serveres' (Wp.A9 160M), we bear left (NW), following a charcoal burners'trail that gradually broadens to a forestry track, descending steadily through successive stretches of healthy oak and sickly pine. Amid a graveyard of pine, we come to another signpost indicating **Font de Dalt** straight ahead and, our route, **Boal de ses Serveres** on the left (170M). Our track, virtually walled in with dead pine, winds down the valley (N) passing occasional wayposts and red waymarks, and running into increasingly erratic GPS reception.

After passing a large *aljub*, the track dwindles to a trail, swinging left (W) and descending steadily, passing another signpost (180M) before bearing right again (NNE), bringing the eastern limits of **Estellencs** into view. We continue descending and, just when it seems we'll soon be tipping into the sea, we come to a signpost indicating we leave the main trail, which descends on the right to **Son Fortuny** (painted in red on a rock), and bear left on a minor trail (190M). We now climb below the **Es Moro** cliffs, where our trail narrows to a path dipping up and down before eventually climbing to a waypost (Wp.A10 205M). Bearing left on a broadening trail, we join the end of the dirt track climbed at the start of the walk, five minutes from the **Boal de ses Serveres** refuge, twenty minutes from the C710.

(b) Puigpunyent: Galatzó from the South

Access: by car

To reach the start, from km 11.1 of the PMV1032 (100 metres west of **Puigpunyent** church, Wp.B1) take the **Camí de sa Teulera** north, more obviously signposted 'La Reserva', setting the odometer at zero. Follow the signs for **La Reserva** to a triple junction at km 3.2 in front of a house called **Es Cucui** (Wp.B2). The **La Reserva** route descends to the left here, but we stay on the main lane, passing a quarry at km 4.2 (Wp.B3). Park at km 4.7 at the bottom of a dirt track forking right. N.B. if there's no room here, stay on the lane and turn right at km 5 on a steep, narrow lane leading to Wp.B5.

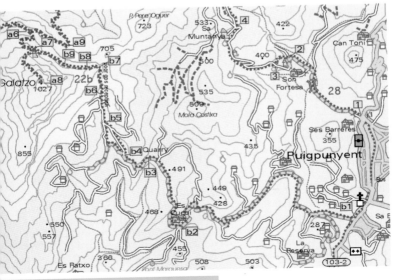

The track (Wp.B4 0M), which is marked with a large mustard dot after twenty metres, climbs steadily for 150 metres before levelling out on tarmac. When the main lane doubles back to the southeast, we maintain a northerly direction for one hundred metres to a U-bend (Wp.B5 10M), where we leave the lane and take a broad, rough track climbing northwest.

(Note we had poor GPS reception between Wps B5-B7.)

After passing a gated branch doubling back on the right, we bear sharp right at a Y-junction and climb a stony trail, at the end of which a waypost and waymarking arrows mark the start of a narrow path (Wp.B6 15M).

The path soon broadens to a trail, climbing steadily through woodland badly battered by storm damage. The woods thin out as we pass the path to the firewatch tower on **Coll des Carniceret** (Wp.B7 25M), after which fine views open out along the eastern ridge of **Es Puntals**, **Planicia** and beyond them, the high **Tramuntana**. We continue our steady climb to the west on a clear path winding through *carritx*, *madroño* and small oak. There are at least two parallel paths here, but all converge at a waypost on a rocky shoulder (Wp.B8 35M), from where we can see a grassy slope to the north of the main summit with what appears to be a cross silhouetted against the skyline.

El Bisbe from the south

Aiming for the 'cross' (in fact a signpost), we follow a narrow but clear path along the northeastern flank of the mountain. The path descends slightly to cross a spill of large boulders (Wp.B9 45M), which are reasonably stable but still require some care. We now have a long, steady climb passing below the distinctive pillar of **El Bisbe** (The Bishop) to the 'cross' signpost next to the foundations of a small hut (Wp.A7 55M).

Bearing left (SW), we follow Version (a). Wps. A7-A8 to the top, after which we return the same way.

A somewhat grandiose title sounding like the trading name of a mercantile league in the middle ages, but in fact the catchall heading for three short walks taking us off the more commonly beaten tourist trail. The 'ports' in question would count as little more than creeks anywhere else and one wouldn't even qualify as that, but on the northern coast with its sheer cliffs and shipwrecking rocks any tiny shelter was welcome and was soon dignified with the name of a port. Nowadays the old imperative of maintaining sea-contact with the outside world has waned and these three tiny 'ports' are virtually abandoned, used only by a few fishermen and the occasional sun-seeking local at weekends. For the rambler in need of a bathe, they are a godsend.

The itineraries are all strolls and should not be thought of as full scale walks. Rather, they are comparable to the southern **Camís de Calvià**, except in this case, given the steeper terrain, I'd recommend them as pre rather post-prandial strolls. Take your swimming costume.

(a) Estellencs

Access: on foot from **Estellencs**

From the western end of **Estellencs**, next to the **Bar-Restaurante Maristel**, we take the old **Andratx** road, signposted 'Platja and Cementiri' (Wp.A1 0M). The road, which is driveable but rarely driven, soon leaves the built up area and narrows to a lane, generally known as the **Camí des Port**. At the junction with the cemetery lane (Wp.A2), we bear right, soon winding through an agreeably shady stretch before descending past the last scattered *casetas* to a stairway (Wp.A3 20M) leading to the stony beach.

After bathing and maybe having a drink in the beach bar if it's open, we continue along the lane as it climbs steeply behind the beach, passing a small parking area (Wp.A4). The gradient soon eases and the lane becomes the **Camí del Mar**, from where we have fine views up the valley to the summit of **Galatzó**.

Estellencs port

After climbing steadily past attractive houses (Wps. A5, A6 & A7) and neatly tended terraces, the lane bears right, crossing a bridge over the torrent (Wp.A8) and passing the large **Es Fonollar** farmhouse (Wp.A9) before a final brief climb brings us back into the village.

Maintaining direction past **Can Llimona**, we fork right on **Carrer Po** then take the next left to join the main road in front of the restaurant **Montimar**, a firm favourite with visitors and locals alike.

(b) Sa Pedre de s'Ase

Access: by car and bus

View west on the descent to Sa Pedre de s'Ase

This itinerary is so blindingly simple it's barely a ramble at all, merely following a narrow lane down to the coast then turning round and coming back up again. But it's not a lane you'd be in a hurry to reverse out of, not if you valued your clutch, so unless you have access to one of the private parking bays en route, I strongly discourage motorists from venturing down here in their cars.

More importantly though, it descends to one of the most delightful little 'ports' on the island and one largely unknown to the hundreds of people who stop everyday at the **Torre des Verger**.

The walk starts near km 89.6 of the C710 between **Estellencs** and **Banyalbufar**, 100 metres west of the **Torre des Verger** (said to be the finest *mirador* along the coast and certainly worth exploring, preferably earlier in the morning before the crowds arrive). There's a bus-stop here (nameless, but

Torre des Verger is well-known) and several parking lay-bys. Between the largest lay-by and the bus-stop, we take a narrow lane (Wp.B1 0M) descending south-west.

The lane passes several attractive *casetas* then veers sharp right in front of two tracks leading to private houses (Wp.B2). At the end of the lane, steps lead down to the superb little 'port' (Wp.B3 25M), a slipway shielded from the sea by two tall rocks and a wall.

It's a great place for bathing in calm weather, though make sure there aren't any of the small brown jellyfish floating about. Locals agree that they give a nasty sting, though there is some dispute as to whether the effects last several days or several months! We return the same way.

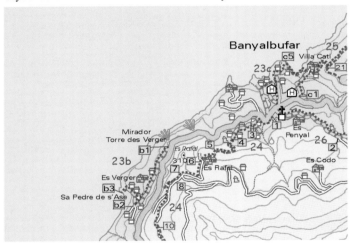

(c) Banyalbufar

Access: on foot from **Banyalbufar**

The walk starts towards the eastern end of **Banyalbufar** in front to the **Hotel Mar i Vent** (Wp.C1 0M). We descend **Carrer Major** and take the first turning on the right, **Carrer Marina**. Veering sharp left at a junction in front of the cemetery (Wp.C2), we leave the village precincts on the **Camí de sa Galera**, a roughly surfaced lane.

The lane descends steeply across terraces of well-maintained vegetable gardens then climbs very briefly to a dirt track, blocked to traffic by a small metal barrier (Wp.C3). Turning left, we follow the stairway down to a narrow ledge running along the left of the slipway, beyond which a concrete causeway leads onto the tiny beach (Wp.C4 15M).

Crossing the beach, we follow more stairs up to a high, railed ledge, where we pass the remains of an old watermill. The ledge path leads to the end of a tarmac lane, the **Camí des Molí** (Wp.C5). Before climbing back to the village, it's worth bearing right onto the low cliff-top parking area, from where we have fine views along the coast and back into the bay.

Banyalbufar port

Returning to the **Camí des Moli**, we follow the lane as it climbs steadily back to the village. Maintaining direction on **Carrer del Pont**, we pass under an archway before rejoining the main road in front of the *ayuntamiento* (Wp.C6 40M).

Our second exception to the 'no controversy' rule is this exquisite stretch of the GR221 traversing olive terraces and oak woods on the lower slopes of the **Planícia** massif. In an effort to cut this ancient right of way, the English owners of the **Es Rafal** estate have posted a host of intimidating notices, and effaced all waymarks, wayposts and cairns on their property. However, the local authorities are fighting back and, for the duration of the court case, the judge has ordered that the path remain open. Since this could last ten years, by which time I hope to have revised several editions of this book(!), there's little risk in publishing the walk.

It would be a terrible shame if such a lovely itinerary were lost to the public and, given that the menace comes from our fellow countrymen, it seems only fair that visiting English ramblers should do their bit to maintain a right of way established by generations of Mallorcans. Having said all that, if you are intimidated by the notices, the best part of the walk (between Wps.11&15) is uncontested and can be done as a linear two-way route in reverse (see Wp.15 below).

** 1 hour 40 mins - 2 hours
* in **Estellencs** at the **Restaurant Montimar** (linear one-way)

Access: on foot from **Banyalbufar**

Starting from the **Restaurante Son Tomás** at the western limit of **Banyalbufar** (Wp.1 0M), we follow the C710 for a little over one hundred metres, passing the **Baronia** car-park, then turn left on a narrow lane (Wp.2), signposted 'GR221 Estellencs 2h20' and 'Camí d'es Rafal Sa Costa'. Forking right one hundred metres later (Wp.3), we follow the lane until it becomes a concrete track, climbing steeply past the houses of **Na Revolta** and **Sa Costa**. The track then dwindles to an intermittently stepped path (Wp.4 15M) climbing to the large green gates of **Es Rafal** (Wp.5 20M).

If these gates are locked, it means the court case is lost and we have to turn back. Otherwise, all the signs are simply an attempt to create a *de facto* impasse regardless of the legal situation. I confess, it's not a very comfy feeling ignoring so much prohibition, but it is worth it. Judging by personal experience and reports from other ramblers, you will not be challenged, while the dog they warn of is restricted to the roof of the house and does no more than bark. However, given that all waymarks have been effaced, you may wish to study the following paragraph closely before proceeding.

Seventy-five metres after the gate, we pass between the house and a threshing circle, and bear left on a track (Wp.6) running SSW. The track curves round the head of a terraced valley then swings sharp left to a Y-junction (Wp.7 30M), where we fork right. This branch track circles a broad terrace used for logging and descends to a junction with a trail climbing from the woods (Wp.8 32M). Turning left, we ignore a minor branch descending to the right ninety metres later* (Wp.9) and follow the main terrace track, climbing slightly as the track dwindles to a trail leading to another unlocked gate (Wp.10 40M), where we leave **Es Rafal** and enter the **Planícia** estate.

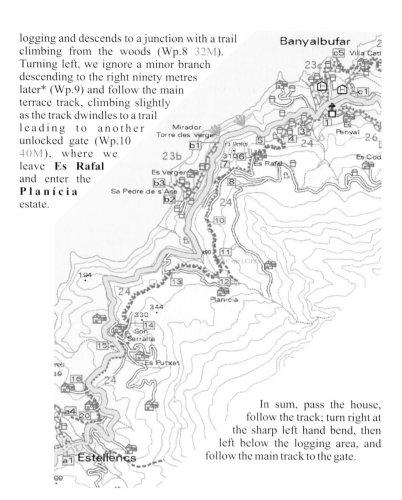

In sum, pass the house, follow the track; turn right at the sharp left hand bend, then left below the logging area, and follow the main track to the gate.

* The branch on the right descends to locked green gates beyond which is the **Font des Garbell**. This lovely spot was a popular picnic area in the past, but given the locked gates, I cannot recommend this diversion.

Wayposts reappear here and only after Wp.15 is a description really helpful, so you may wish to put the book away now and simply enjoy the finest part of the walk. All junctions until Wp.15 are clearly signposted. Four hundred metres after the gate, the trail swings south to an immense, dead pine, just short of the stagnant **Font de s'Obi** and a small cabin.

The cabin near Font de s'Obi

Immediately before the dead pine (Wp.11 50M), we turn right on a rough path descending through the woods to cross the **Torrent de Can Cerdà**, immediately after which, we fork left (Wp.12).

This stage of the walk is pure pleasure, winding through a wood of healthy oak, the path dappled with sunlight and dead leaves, and not a prohibition panel in sight! The oak are replaced by pine as we approach then cross the **Planícia** farm access road (Wp.13 65M). We then traverse a small rise and follow a pleasant corniche path winding between pine set against the azure blue sea. After going through a gateway in a wall, the path curves south and joins a dirt track (Wp.14 75M) above the fine old manor house of **Son Serralta**, the history of which dates back to the thirteenth century. The track descends to **Son Serralta**'s concrete driveway, which we follow down to the C710 near km 92.2 (Wp.15 80M)

This is the starting point for the reverse, non-controversial route. The path to **Font de s'Obi** is clear and well-signposted and requires no detailed description. One hundred metres west of Wp.15, there's a narrow lane to the south, at the mouth of which there's room for one carefully parked car. Allow 2-2½ hours (return).

We now follow the C710 for 600 metres. Although it's not busy, this is the main northern road, so take care, walking on the left side of the road and standing well back when the occasional car passes. Curving through a sharp left-hand bend, we pass the 800-metre kilometre stone and turn right (Wp.16 87M) on a narrow path descending to a bend in a lane (Wp.17), where we turn left on a stretch of the old royal way.

Galatzó behind Ses Amitges

At a bend in a narrow, partially concreted track, we bear left (Wp.18), passing directly in front of another grand house, **Ses Amitges**. We then cross a second, narrow, concrete track and pass under a lovely, shady fig tree, joining a third concrete track (Wp.19) which we follow to the right, rejoining the C710 at the eastern limit of **Estellencs** (Wp.20 95M).

The bus-stop is at the western end of the village.

The **Camí des Pescadors** or Fishermen's Path and the **Camí Sa Volta des General**, The General's Tour, named after the local aristocrat for whom it was constructed, are two of the great 'commuting' paths of the northwest and combine to make a near perfect day's hiking, including fabulous sea views, charming woodland paths, a wild coastline, a grand manor house, daunting cliffs and a good dose of domesticity in the welcome guise of the bars and restaurants of **Port des Canonge** and **Banyalbufar**. I say 'almost' because it's a linear walk and I prefer circuits, but if you're feeling energetic this minor imperfection can be remedied by returning to **Esporles** on the **Camí des Correu** (see Walk 26). For the most part, the route is well wayposted.

4 🚶	3¾-4H	13 km	〽️ 350m / 480m	⟺	5 🍴

Access: on foot from **Esporles**, return via the 15.45 bus or via Walk 26

Esporles

Starting in front of **Esporles** church (Wp.1 0M), we take **Carrer Nou San Pere**, crossing the *torrent* of the same name and **Carrer Major**. The next turning on the left, **Carrer Pont**, leads briefly into **Carrer de Sa Costeta**, where we bear left on **Carrer de sa Pansa**, the nameplate of which is partially obscured by ivy.

We then turn right on **Carrer s'Avenc**, which ends in a car-park (Wp.2 10M) where we take a dirt track to the north.

Ignoring all branches, we follow the main track as it climbs gently across the **Costa de son Dameto**. At a Y-junction where there's a large rock in the crux of the Y with 'Es Noguera' painted on it (Wp.3 30M), we bear left, staying on the main track. The track climbs past scattered cottages and cabins, passing a branch for **Can Covent** (Wp.4), after which it dwindles to a trail leading to a triple junction of tracks (Wp.5 50M). Ignoring a concrete track descending to the left, we bear left along the main dirt track, passing the entrance to **Can Pastor**. Forking left 100 metres later (Wp.6), we descend behind a house to a path that leads to the C710 (Wp.7 55M).

Turning left we follow the road for fifty metres, passing the km 79 post. At a wayposted crossroads (Wp.8) with a dirt track just below a blue 40km speed limit sign, we turn right on the branch of the track heading north. Near the start

and at the end of this track you will see small 'Camino Privado Prohibido El Paso' signs. Ignore these. This is a well-used, official path, wayposted by the local authorities, and residents en route assured us there was no problem. At the end of the track, we go through a gate to the walled area and small *mirador* at **Mirant del Mar** (Wp.9 75M).

Thirty metres to the left of the *mirador* and again in the far corner, breaches in the wall lead to a narrow dirt path descending gently through the woods (SW) before veering west and steepening. Joining the lane down to **Port des Canonge** (Wp.10 85M), we follow the road to the right, snaking through a tight chicane, at the tail of which, we take a wayposted path doubling back to the left (Wp.11 95M). This is perhaps the loveliest part of the **Camí des Pescadors** as we descend through the **Son Coll** woods, principally oak, but also pine and laurel. On reaching a bend in a broad trail (Wp.12 105M), we continue descending to join a dirt track, also on a bend (Wp.13 110M). Twenty metres to the left, a waypost indicates a slithery descent to recover the path as it runs alongside a dry torrent. At the junction with the next dirt track (Wp.14 115M), we turn right to rejoin the tarmac road fifty metres later. We now follow the road down to the coast, passing en route the **Can Madó** and **Can Toni Moreno** restaurants.

At the T-junction above the bay (Wp.15 130M), we turn left down to the parking area, from the end of which, we can see, seventy-five metres to the left, an isolated signpost indicating 'Banyalbufar 1h20'. Bearing left through the gateway at the end of the car-park, we follow the signposted route, crossing a small gully and climbing through the woods behind the seafront.

After descending into a second, larger gully lined with abandoned fishermen's shanties, we climb a short flight of steps, beyond which wayposts lead us through a maze of interlinking tracks, trails and paths to join the end of a very broad dirt track in front of double wooden gates (Wp.16 140M).

We follow this dirt track west, towards the **Es Corral Fals** cliffs, climbing steadily along the boundary line of the **Son Bunyola** estate, now owned by Richard Branson. Within sight of the immense manor house (so very immense one can only pray the man has lots of friends), we bear right at a Y-junction (Wp.17 155M). One hundred and fifty metres later, having already passed a first branch on the left, we bear right at a triple junction (Wp.18) to follow a broad signposted trail curving round below the bulging cliffs of **Es Corral Fals** from where we have superb views over the **Punta de s'Àguila**.

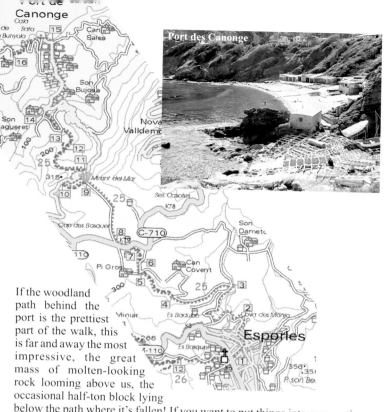

Port des Canonge

If the woodland path behind the port is the prettiest part of the walk, this is far and away the most impressive, the great mass of molten-looking rock looming above us, the occasional half-ton block lying below the path where it's fallen! If you want to put things into perspective or feel the need to dwarf human vanity, come here and scurry past quickly - you feel very small, indeed.

After that humbling little passage, our route becomes a classic Mallorcan corniche trail. Strolling through pine woods backed by the deep blue sea (green and blue really ought to be the colours of the island's flag), we pass a lime-kiln (Wp.19 175M) and a small ruin (Wp.20 190M). Ignoring a major trail descending toward the coast, we go through old iron gates, 150 metres after which, directly behind the house of **Sa Cabarola**, we leave the main trail (Wp.21 200M).

The main trail leads round to the **Volta des General** bend in the C710, a popular starting point for the descent to **Port des Canonge**, but to avoid a kilometre on the main road, we turn sharp right behind **Sa Cabarola** on a narrow path initially heading in a northerly direction. The path then zigzags down (SW) to a sharp right hand bend (Wp.22 205M), where we descend onto a well trodden way winding steeply through palmetto, *carritx* and pine to join a narrow track directly behind a flat-roofed house overlooking **Port de Banyalbufar** (Wp.23 215M). Bearing left, we join a roughly surfaced lane, the **Camí de sa Galera**, which we follow up to the village. After a brief steep climb, we reach the main road in front of the **Hotel Mar i Vent** (Wp.24 225M). The bus-stop and the start of the **Camí des Correu** (Walk 26) are two hundred metres to the west.

The 'Mail Path' between **Banyalbufar** and **Esporles** is another of Mallorca's great commuting routes and, combined with Walk 25, makes for one of the most memorable day-long walks on the island. However, I count it as a discrete itinerary as the climb out of **Banyalbufar** is steep and can seem interminable on a hot afternoon. If you feel up to it, combine the two. If in doubt, use the bus and enjoy two half-day excursions. The **Camí des Correu** has now been incorporated in the **GR221** and was restored a few years ago. With one notable exception, all major junctions are well signposted and, once you're on-trail, description is virtually superfluous, which is all to the good, since the path crosses some of the loveliest oak woods on the island, and it would be a shame to be reading about it rather than simply enjoying it.

Access: on foot from **Banyalbufar**   *in **Esporles**

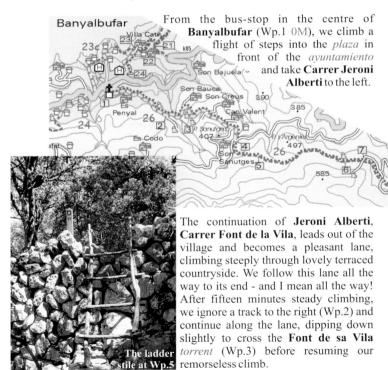

From the bus-stop in the centre of **Banyalbufar** (Wp.1 0M), we climb a flight of steps into the *plaza* in front of the *ayuntamiento* and take **Carrer Jeroni Alberti** to the left.

The continuation of **Jeroni Alberti**, **Carrer Font de la Vila**, leads out of the village and becomes a pleasant lane, climbing steeply through lovely terraced countryside. We follow this lane all the way to its end - and I mean all the way! After fifteen minutes steady climbing, we ignore a track to the right (Wp.2) and continue along the lane, dipping down slightly to cross the **Font de sa Vila** *torrent* (Wp.3) before resuming our remorseless climb.

The ladder stile at Wp.5

Ten minutes later, we pass a small vineyard and, five minutes after that, a signposted entrance to **Can Valent**, welcome harbingers of the lane's eventual end. After climbing 'forever', we come to the end of the lane at a major junction of tracks and trails (Wp.4 35M) on the edge of the **Son Sanutges** estate.

Forking right on a signposted trail between two dirt tracks, we join the **Camí des Correu** proper, climbing more gently to cross a tumbledown wall and, fifty metres later, a second wall with a ladder stile (Wp.5 45M). After a brief level stretch, the trail, which is cobbled with large rocks, burrows through the woods, climbing gently before levelling out again. This stretch of the trail is dirt and is lined with tall pine, through which we can glimpse the **Teix** massif behind **Valldemossa** and, way below us (way, way below us if we passed it earlier in the morning!) the **Son Bunyola** estate.

We now follow a contour line, passing a lime kiln (Wp.6 60M), shortly after which we cross a narrow dirt track (Wp.7 65M). Five minutes later we cross another, very faint track below a mossy *sitja* and then cross a third wall, after which we begin our gentle, winding descent to **Esporles**, forty minutes away according to the sign, an estimate that seems to expand as we descend. Two hundred and fifty metres beyond the third wall, after a series of zigzags, the trail appears to double back to the left, continuing its zigzagging descent away from what looks like the end of a broad dirt track (Wp.8 80M) N.B. This is the only major junction en route not clearly signposted. In fact, we ignore the branch to the left and continue (S) on the 'dirt track' toward a wall.

The 'track' soon dwindles to a cobbled trail again, passing a waypost fifty metres later. The trail runs parallel to the wall, passing another kiln before descending to a wire gate through the wall (Wp.9 90M). Descending alongside abandoned olive terraces, we go through another wall gate, five minutes after which we reach the PM110 (Wp.10 102M), just above **Sa Granja** and the junction with the PMV1101. Crossing the road, we follow the new, clearly signposted path running alongside the PM110, which isn't particularly pretty, but is a considerable improvement on the kilometre of road-walking this route previously entailed.

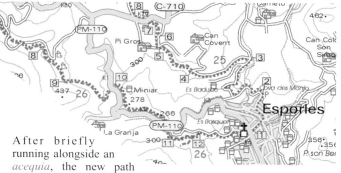

After briefly running alongside an *acequia*, the new path descends to a bend of the old road, fifty metres after which we cross onto a narrow, initially asphalted track with wooden gates (Wp.11 117M). After crossing a small rise and going through a second gateway (Wp.12), a stepped descent debouches on the **Costa de Sant Pere** lane, which we follow down to the back of the church, where we bear left for the main road. The **Café Deportiu** is one hundred metres to the south, the bus stop is on **Carrer Jaume I**, a turning on the right fifty metres after the café.

The **Fita del Ram** is the highest point on the heavily wooded massif between **Esporles** and **Puigpunyent**, an area that was once a vital source of charcoal, as a result of which the mountain is crisscrossed with charcoal burners' paths and speckled with hundreds of *sitjes*.

There are several ways up the **Fita del Ram** (*fita* means landmark, Ram, literally 'bunch' or 'bouquet', was the name of the family who owned the land in the eighteenth century), but in this instance we stick to the best known and consequently best waymarked route via the **Ermita de Maristel**. I say 'best known', yet the itinerary rarely features in guidebooks, which is baffling as this lovely woodland walk should be on every rambler's must-do list. You've got to like getting away from it all, though; the top's not very wild, but it is very isolated. Pathfinding near the end requires a certain amount of concentration, but is not dauntingly complex.

Motorists can cut fifty minutes from the full itinerary by driving to the **Son Ferra** estate (turn left for 'Es Verger / Área Recreativa Son Tries' as you arrive in **Esporles** from the south, immediately setting the odometer at zero; the narrow gate at Wp.7 is at km 2.3), though I don't particularly recommend this, as the path out of **Esporles** is an attractive one in its own right.

*   but allow 5 hours

Access: on foot from **Esporles**

For the full itinerary, we also take the **Es Verger** road (Wp.1 0M), but turn left at the first crossroads. Carrying straight on at the next crossroads (no nameplate, though we're following **Carrer des Quarter**), we pass the *Guardia Civil* barracks, then turn right at the next junction (onto **Carrer des Rafal**), passing houses N°s 17 & 19. When the road swings left and descends back towards the PM104, we maintain direction on a narrow track between stone walls (Wp.2 6M).

The track climbs through a cluster of houses, crossing a small rise, after which we turn right (Wp.3 10M) behind an old house half painted white. We go through a wicker and wire gate, then follow a pleasant terrace path curving round to a T-junction (Wp.4 15M), where we again turn right on a path climbing alongside the narrow, partially tailored channel of a *torrent*.

After a second wicker and wire gate, we join a dirt track (Wp.5 20M) which we follow back to the **Es Verger** road. Forty metres up the road (Wp.6) we turn left on a narrow, overgrown, roughly paved path, climbing between fenced walls and a host of hedgerow flowers to a surfaced track just below the **Es Verger** road. On the far side of the road is a small gate, behind which a large carob tree overshadows the *ermita* path (Wp.7 30M).

The main gate is locked, but a narrow one-person-wide entrance lets us squeeze through onto the path, our route confirmed by a hand-painted 'ERMITA' sign shortly after the carob tree. The path almost immediately joins a narrow track climbing to the right of the **Son Ferra** farmhouse (Wp.8), behind which we go through (and shut!) a gate.

Son Ferra at Wp.8

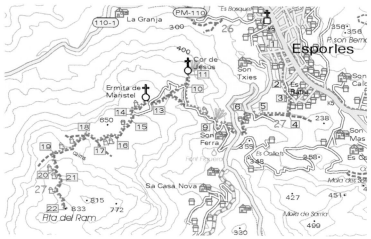

El Cor de Jesús at Wp.11

Climbing into the woods, the track runs parallel to then crosses an old trail, immediately after which we go through another gate. The track, which is mainly concreted here, climbs steeply through the woods. At a second gap in the concrete there is a small, very flimsily fenced *mirador* off to the right (Wp.9 45M). After the next and final stretch of concrete ends, the gradient eases then levels off altogether, passing two faint charcoal-burners' paths off to the left. We then climb gently (N) to a sharp left-hand bend, where a broad trail branches right (Wp.10 62M) leading in one hundred metres to the **El Cor de Jesús** statue/*mirador* (Wp.11) overlooking **Esporles**.

Returning to Wp.10 (72M), we continue up the track for less than 100 metres to a clear, cairn-marked shortcut (Wp.12) joining one of the paths passed after the end of the concrete.

Ermita de Maristel

Turning right, we follow this path, crossing a wall and passing a cave, before rejoining the track just below the **Ermita de Maristel** (Wp.13 83M). The *ermita* dates from 1888 and is of no great architectural interest, but the superb location confirms once again that the rewards of a religious vocation are worldly as well as heavenly.

On the far side of the grassy clearing to the south of the *ermita*, we go through a gap in a wall and follow a cairn-marked trail to the right alongside another wall. The trail meanders through the woods, crossing the end of another broad trail between two *sitjes* (Wp.14), at which point the cairns guide us onto a narrow path winding between low outcrops of rock.

Passing a tiny, mossy *aljub* and crossing a wall (Wp.15 94M), we come to a second clearing where a small cabin is currently being restored. At the end of the clearing, we climb back into the woods, bearing right to cross a wall (Wp.16), after which the trail levels off in a particularly delightful area of woodland where the oak and strawberry trees are more evenly intermingled.

Seventy-five metres after a lime-kiln, we ignore a minor branch on the left (Wp.17) and continue on the main trail, passing a grassy roofed reservoir (Wp.18 102M), beyond which we ignore a turning to the right and climb through a chicane before resuming our pleasant, level stroll.

We stick to the main trail (if you happen to see cairns on the left next to a rock marked with a red cross, ignore them) until it climbs to a breach in a wall (Wp.19 110M). Immediately after crossing the wall, we leave the main trail which descends SW, and turn left (SE) as indicated by cairns and faint waymarks. There are long stretches of reasonably clear path here, but it often disappears in bare rock, so it's important to follow the cairn-marked route for the rest of the climb.

In a further seventy-five metres, the cairns lead us through a natural passage between two large outcrops of rocks, after which we continue climbing parallel to the wall crossed at Wp.19. A little under 100 metres after the natural passage, we veer away from the wall (SSW), and continue our steady climb to a *sitja* (Wp.20 122M). Red waymarks appear to mark a route off to the right, but we stay with the cairns, climbing to the left of the *sitja* (W) on a relatively clear path, passing twin *sitjes* fifty metres later.

Behind the twin *sitjes* are what appear to be the rocks of the summit. They ain't! After going up a rocky way to the north of the false summit, we climb behind it, crossing a tumbledown wall (Wp.21 127M) linking it with another large outcrop, again not the summit. A *sitja* beyond the wall marks the start of another reasonably clear path (SW), passing a second *sitja* and bisecting a third, 150 metres after which a narrow chute blocked with natural steps leads to the trig-point on the summit (Wp.22 138M).

'Summit' is a somewhat grand term for a tiny hump of rock just poking over the treetops, but whatever you call it, it's one of those places you won't regret visiting. The views are predictably superb, stretching from **Massanella** in the east to **Galatzó** in the west, but more beguiling still is the immediate landscape, a magical, peaceful tangle of twisty-trunked oaks rimed with hanks of lichen, the occasional ghostly shadow of an unseen seagull gliding overhead, the only sound being bird song, the hum of insects, and the occasional patter of a falling leaf.

Galatzó as seen from the summit

We descend almost by the same route, carefully following the cairns back to Wp.19 and, after Wp.15, forking left on the narrower path rather than taking the broad trail that presents itself straight ahead. The only difference is that, once on the shortcut path passing the cave below the *ermita*, we stay on the main path to emerge on the dirt track below rather than above Wp.10.

The *puntals* of **Son Fortesa** and **Son Balaguer** are two small summits flanked by sheer cliffs on the long ridge linking **Galatzó** and the **Planícia** massif. It's a wonderful, little visited area where the peace is absolute, interrupted only by the soughing of the wind, the faint tock of falling leaves, and the chirping of birds - and even they seem to be muted, as if respecting the prevailing hush. The ultimate get-away-from-it-all walk without going into manifestly dangerous wilderness! There are two parts to our version of this itinerary, the first an easy circuit on clearly wayposted charcoal-burners' tracks and trails suitable for all energetic ramblers, the second a linear ascent onto the ridge only recommended for experienced ramblers with good pathfinding skills.

5 | 3½-4 H ** | 12.5 km | 650m / 650m | ↻ | 2*

**   but allow 5 hours
*   in **Puigpunyent**

Access: on foot from **Puigpunyent**

To reach the start from the Carretera PMV1101 **Cantonada Escola** bus-stop in the centre of **Puigpunyent**, head uphill, past the **Restaurant ses Cotxeries**, bearing left after 600 metres on the **Carretera Nova d'Estellencs**. The walk starts two hundred metres later, just beyond the town limits at a sharp right hand bend immediately before the 1 kilometre post. Motorists should park in the broad residential street on the left (signposted 'La Reserva') next to the town limit sign.

As the road swings sharp right beside a walking signpost for **Es Grau** (Wp.1 0M) we maintain direction (NW) on a stony track leading to a gated tarmac lane where there are signs prohibiting cars, motorbikes and cyclists.

The Son Fortesa lane

This delightful lane, flanked by masses of wildflowers, curves across a small rise then descends to cross a bridge before climbing alongside the high eastern wall of the **Son Fortesa** manor house.

As the lane curves round to approach the house from the northeast, two tracks fork off to the right (Wp.2 15M). The main track climbs through the farm buildings behind **Son Fortesa**, but we take the easternmost, gated track, signposted 'Camí Vell d'Estellencs'. The track, which is overgrown, climbs to a bedstead gate, then veers left to join the main track from the farm buildings

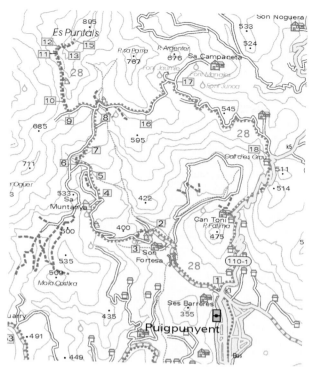

(Wp.3 20M), on which we bear right. All subsequent junctions until Wp.8 are clearly indicated by cairns, waymarks and wayposts.

The track climbs steadily, passing a large reservoir and running alongside a tiny, gutter-like *acequia*. At a sharp right-hand bend, we take a wayposted shortcut (Wp.SC1-SC2), rejoining the track a minute later within sight of the abandoned **Sa Muntanya** farmhouse. We continue on the track, climbing across terraces of gnarled and blasted olive trees, passing a tunneled spring just below the house. The track then doubles back to the left, passing a rough branch down to the house and another branch climbing NNW (Wp.4 41M). We stay on the main track as it veers right, crossing a wall, after which we ignore a faint trail marked with a cairn on the left. Forking left at a Y-junction, we climb to a bend in another track where we bear right (Wp.5 45M).

Climbing into dense oak forest, the track crosses a second wall, fifty metres after which it veers left and we branch right on a minor, wayposted trail (Wp.6 50M) running alongside the wall. The trail crosses the end of a branch track before rejoining the main track (Wp.7 54M), which we follow to the right (ENE), climbing to a signposted T-junction (Wp.8 67M). To return to **Puigpunyent**, we take the track to the right, signposted 'Es Grau 55M'. To climb onto the **Es Puntals** ridge, we turn left.

The track to the left climbs steadily before levelling out on the heavily wooded **Coll d'Estellencs**, sometimes also called **Es Coll**. Fifty metres after it levels out, we leave the **Camí Vell d'Estellencs**, turning right on a narrow path marked by a large cairn and red waymarks (Wp.9 66M). The path weaves through the woods then climbs steeply to a gateway through a wall (Wp.10 82M), after which the sea and **Estellencs** can be seen to the north. The path is very narrow here but clearly defined by large banks of *carritx* as it burrows through the woods, climbing gently to pass a *sitja* and ruined hut. After following a contour where we have to duck under overhanging boughs, the path climbs again and becomes more obscure in the absence of defining *carritx*, obliging us to look out for the cairns and waymarks. It then descends slightly passing below a second *sitja* (Wp.11 93M), discernible from below by the unnaturally flat line of its rim.

Immediately after this second *sitja*, look up to the right and you will see cairns and red waymarks indicating a route climbing through the woods. The remaining climb is off path and it's essential to follow the way/cairn-marked route as its all too easy to become disoriented in the sun-dappled maze of these dense woods. To confirm you're on the right route, look back at the *sitja* as you climb and you will see the ruins (now little more than windbreak walls) of three huts tucked into the surrounding rocks.

Climbing steeply through the woods on a carpet of leaf mould and pine needles, we come to the nose of a long spur of rock (Wp.12 96M). The cairn-marked route climbs along the western side of this spur. From the crown of the spur (Wp.13 98M) we climb NE toward the summit rocks, just visible through the treetops. From the base of these rocks (Wp.14 102M), we climb very steeply up a slippery slope of rock, loose soil and acorn husks.

After thirty metres we have a choice of routes. To reach the summit itself, bear left for a very steep scramble up a long channel of rock. To be honest, I took one look at this and thought, "I can't be having that"! The scramble up is straightforward enough, but as a descent it would be like trying to be discreet on a greased slide. I suspect its the sort of thing that could only really be recommended to people who would disdain to read a book like this anyway.

Galatzó and S'Esclop seen from Wp.15

Instead, I recommend bearing right and scrambling across bare rock to a mini-summit at the western end of the ridge (Wp.15 107M), from where we can see **Palma**, **Galatzó** and **S'Esclop**. Do not attempt to follow the vertiginous ledge route along the southern side of the ridge.

Having enjoyed the views, we descend by the same route, doubtless on our backsides to begin with. Again, follow the cairns, as the slope is even more disorienting in descent. And stay on the western side of the spur. There is another cairn-marked route on the eastern side, but this leads to the path down to **Banyalbufar**. Also take care between the two *sitjes* as this path is even less obvious when walking east to west

Having returned to Wp.8 (136M), we take the easterly track for **Es Grau**, passing a branch on the left and a large lime-kiln on our right. Ignoring what appears to be a cairn-marked path on the right, we stay on the main track after the lime-kiln, climbing through an S-bend, passing above a *sitja* and small ruin, then fork left at a wayposted junction. The track now gradually dwindles to a trail following a wall that soon converges with another wall where we bear left through a gateway (Wp.16 148M), bringing the **Es Puntals** and **Planicia** cliffs into view.

The trail, which is now partially cobbled, descends across terraces, veering back and forth but on the whole maintaining a generally easterly direction, and bringing the **Teix** and western, antennae-topped end of the **Alfabía** Ridge into view. At a junction with a narrow dirt track, we turn right then right again fifty metres later on the main track (Wp.17 162M), which leads (on the left) to the superbly situated house of **Sa Campaneta**. We now simply follow this track through a series of gates (either open or unlocked) all the way to the **Coll d'es Grau** (Wp.18 187M) and the main road between **Puigpunyent** and **Esporles**.

Perhaps 'main' road is a slight exaggeration. First of all it's the *only* road, second it's rarely more than three strides wide, and thirdly it twists back and forth like an agitated snake, making it better suited for bicycles than cars, all of which is to the good, since this is our route back to **Puigpunyent**. Turning right, we cross the coll and take the first of three wayposted shortcuts that eventually emerge just short of the 3.1 kilometre-post (Wp.19 195M). We now follow the road for 2 kilometres, which isn't ideal, but experience suggests that if you see more than three cars and a handful of cyclists, you're having a bad day. The only really disagreeable stretch is a 100-metre gauntlet guarded by four well-fenced but exceedingly irascible dogs.

Nowadays it would be hard to imagine two communities in such close proximity with so little common economic ground as **Puigpunyent** and **Calvià**, the first of which hardly seems to have an economy at all, while the latter is the administrative hub for the thriving tourist resorts along the southern coast. There's no bus link between the two towns and no direct road, yet they must once have had considerable contact as this itinerary, following the remains of an old donkey trail between the two, illustrates.

It's a lovely route crossing beautiful countryside with fine views, the only drawback being that missing bus link, which entails a round trip via **Palma**. Motorists might park at Wp.4 and do the best bit of the walk between Wps.4&8 as a linear return, otherwise I'm afraid we're on the buses for the day. It's worth the effort though and, if you're feeling energetic, you could combine this itinerary with Walk 6 for a long but easy and very satisfying ramble crossing two thirds of western Mallorca.

Buses for **Puigpunyent** leave **Palma** at 7.55am & 1pm on weekdays, 9am & 2pm on Saturdays, and 9am on Sundays - journey time approximately thirty minutes. The walk is easy to follow and all critical junctions are signposted or wayposted. The road at the start isn't very attractive, but neither is it very busy.

*in **Calvià**

Access: by bus

From the **Carrer sa Travessia** bus-stop in **Puigpunyent** opposite the **Bar/Restaurant Es Pont** (0M), we walk up the PMV1032 toward **Galilea** and **Es Capdella** for 950 metres, until we pass a large stone and ceramic sign for 'Es Eubello', immediately after which we bear right on a signposted track cutting a long bend in the road (Wp.2 14M).

A little over one hundred metres later we rejoin the road, which we follow for another 250 metres, passing the km 10.6 post, after which, at a sharp left-hand bend, we maintain direction (SW) on a wayposted path (Wp.3 20M). The path climbs steadily, crossing a lane to continue on a stepped stretch of the old donkey trail, rejoining the road next to a tiny cottage thirty metres below the **Coll des Molí de Vent**.

Climbing to the *coll*, we bear left in front of the vertical-bar gates of **Son Cortey** (Wp.4 32M) and cross a metal latticework gate via a ladder-stile, immediately veering right on a good dirt track. Five hundred metres later, the main track climbs toward **Na Bauçana** (see Walk 30) and

The sign at Wp.5

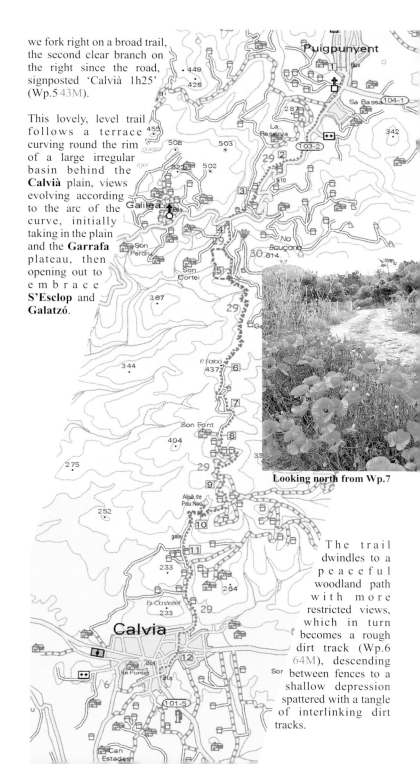

we fork right on a broad trail, the second clear branch on the right since the road, signposted 'Calvià 1h25' (Wp.5 43M).

This lovely, level trail follows a terrace curving round the rim of a large irregular basin behind the **Calvià** plain, views evolving according to the arc of the curve, initially taking in the plain and the **Garrafa** plateau, then opening out to embrace **S'Esclop** and **Galatzó**.

Looking north from Wp.7

The trail dwindles to a peaceful woodland path with more restricted views, which in turn becomes a rough dirt track (Wp.6 64M), descending between fences to a shallow depression spattered with a tangle of interlinking dirt tracks.

Following the wayposted route, we stick to the main track, crossing the depression and climbing to a junction with a better stabilized track (Wp.7 75M). Bearing left, we climb across the rise to a paddock and the gate into the **Son Font Urbanización** (Wp.8 80M).

We now follow a tarmac road (the **Camí de na Morruda**, later the **Camí de Son Font**) as it descends between large villas. At a Y-junction (Wp.9 96M), we bear right on the **Camí des Molí Fariner**, descending 250 metres to a crossroads where we turn right on the **Camí des Pou Nou**. At the end of the lane, we maintain direction (W) on a dirt track that soon dwindles to a trail curving round to a signposted junction of paths (Wp.10 105M). The **Aljub de Pou Nou** (dry but worth visiting) is 100 metres to the north, while the **Calvià** path veers sharp left.

Having visited the *aljub* (not counted in subsequent times), we follow the **Calvià** path as it curves below a small cliff. After crossing a slight rise, the path descends along the course of a valley, broadening once again to become a dirt track and going through a gate (usually open but otherwise passed by stone steps in the wall on the right) before joining a major track (Wp.11 116M). Bearing left, we follow this track down to rejoin the main *urbanización* road a few minutes later.

Turning right, we follow the road into **Calvià**, arriving on the **Carrer de Son Mir**. After forking right at a Y-junction, we turn left on **Carrer Jaume III**, signposted 'Llar des Majors', which joins the main east-west road through **Calvià** next to the **Bar Bodeguilla** (Wp.12 132M). Bearing right then immediately left at the mini-roundabout, we follow **Carrer de Sor Rosenda** down to the **Palma** road. The bus-stop is fifty metres to the left, next to the **Ca Na Cucó Restaurant**.

Buses for **Palmanova** leave at:-
14.20/14.50/15.35/16.05/16.50/17.20/18.20/19.35 & 20.50.

Direct buses to **Palma** leave at:-
13.45/14.20/14.30/18.35 & 19.30.

Walk 6 can be joined by taking the **Capdella** road from the **Bodeguilla** roundabout or, if you get fed up waiting for the bus, by following **Carrer Vicente Chinchilla** from behind the bus-stop to the T-junction with the **Camí de Son Pillo**.

The small peak of **Na Bauçana** (also known as **Bauza**) probably enjoys more prominence per metre than any other summit on the island. Despite it's relatively modest height (614 metres) it's a landmark for miles around, its wooded dome clearly visible from most of our southern itineraries. More importantly in rambling terms, the scope of the views from the top is almost unique, including the **Na Burguesa** ridge, the **Garrafa** plateau, the peaks behind **Sa Trapa**, **S'Esclop**, **Galatzó**, **Es Puntals**, **Planicia**, the **Fita del Ram** - in fact, just about everything all the way to **Puig Major** and **Massanella** in the east. Hardly any other viewing point boasts quite such an encompassing outlook. The walk is mainly on good dirt tracks and only earns a high exertion rating for the steep path at the end.

Access: by car and (if you insist) bus - see note below

The walk starts at the entrance to the **Son Cortey** estate on the **Coll des Molí de Vent** at km 8.3 of the PMV1032 between **Puigpunyent** and **Galilea**. There's parking for one car immediately west of the **Son Cortey** gate and two to the east. If you don't have private transport, you *could* reach the start by taking the **Puigpunyen**t bus from **Palma** (7.55am & 1pm weekdays, 9am & 2pm Saturdays, and 9am on Sundays). I emphasize *could*, as you have to phone and book the previous day (971-614-095) if the bus is to continue to

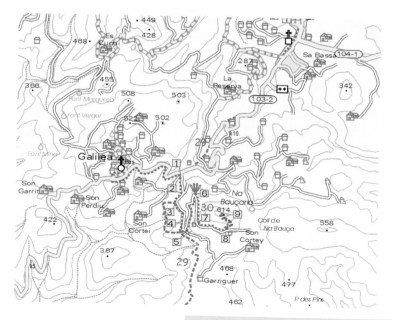

Galilea, from where you would have to walk back down the **Puigpunyent** road for 1 kilometre. You could ask the driver to drop you off at **Coll des Molí de Vent**, but I doubt he'd be willing on such a narrow road. If you do take the bus, combine this itinerary with Walk 29 down to **Calvià** where there's a more regular service for the end of the day.

Ignoring the double-gates of the entrance into **Son Cortey**, we take a track on the left marked with a walking signpost for 'Calvià' and blocked to vehicles by a metal latticework gate (Wp.1 0M). We cross the gate via a ladder stile, then immediately veer right, after which we maintain a southerly direction at an inverted Y-junction (Wp.2) and ignore a branch descending to the right (Wp.3). At the next Y-junction (Wp.4 11M), the **Calvià** trail forks right (signposted 'Calvià 1h25'), but we stay on the main track. Seventy-five metres later we double back to the left (Wp.5 the track straight ahead is ornamented with a sign explicitly prohibiting walkers), climbing NNE.

The track passes two lime-kilns and becomes narrower as it climbs through an extraordinary profusion of strawberry trees. At a natural *mirador* overlooking **Galilea** (Wp.6), the track veers back to the south-east, soon passing a narrow, cairn-marked path (Wp.7 27M) on the right descending ten metres to a well-preserved charcoal burners' hut with an unusual, paved *sitja*. Curving round to the south of **Na Bauçana**, we cross a wall and pass a second cabin/*sitja* as we climb across a grassy rise. Shortly after passing a large waymarking arrow pieced together from rocks, we leave the track, forking left (Wp.8 38M) on a clearly defined cairn-marked trail (NNE).

The stepped path to the summit

The trail soon dwindles to a path, climbing steeply through the woods, crossing frequent steps of roughly tailored stone. In case you're wondering what such a well-made path is doing going nowhere very practical, this itinerary dates from the early nineteenth century when rambling or *excursionisme* was integral to resurgent Catalán and Mallorcan nationalisms, a means of both expressing identity and claiming one's homeland, in the course of which many classic rambling routes were either trailblazed or tailored, including **Massanella**, **Sa Trapa**, **Puig Tomir**, **Puig d'en Farineta**, the **Pas Vermell** and the present itinerary.

After a steady to steep climb, we eventually wind across bare rock to the trig-point (Wp.9 52M) for views that give the lie to the summit's diminutive size. We return by the same route.

GPS Waypoints for the 30 walking routes included in Walk! Mallorca West are quoted in Latitude/Longitude for the WGS84 Datum; the default datum for GPS receivers. Before loading waypoints into your GPS unit please read 'Using GPS in Mallorca' on page 24.

To input the waypoints into your GPS set the 'location format' to 'hddd°.mm.mmm´ and check that your datum is set to WGS84. While we quote waypoints to four places of decimals, as recorded during our research, you might only be able to input to three places of decimals, depending upon your GPS unit. In this case round the third decimal place to the nearest number; e.g. .0178 would be rounded to .018, while .9224 would be rounded to .922.

Full GPS Track and Waypoint files for these 30 walking routes, in Oziexplorer format files, are available on our PNFs (Personal Navigator Files) CD Version 2.01 available for £7.99 from Discovery Walking Guides Ltd. See our websites for more information:-

www.walking.demon.co.uk and www.dwgwalking.co.uk

1.
SERRA DE SON CAMPS: PUJOL DES GAT

Wp	N	E
1	39 36.1302	2 34.2348
2	39 36.0216	2 34.6674
3	39 35.9046	2 34.3674
4	39 35.5590	2 34.0056
5	39 35.4354	2 33.9084
6	39 35.4204	2 33.8082
7	39 34.9206	2 33.7950

2.
NA BURGUESA: MIRADOR DE N'ALZAMORA

Wp	N	E
1	39 34.8216	2 33.7422
2	39 34.4760	2 34.0038
3	39 34.3812	2 33.6150
4	39 34.2120	2 33.3756
5	39 34.2270	2 33.0972
6	39 34.0014	2 33.7734
7	39 33.9558	2 34.0464

3.
NA BURGUESA: TOUR OF PUIG GROS DE BENDINAT

Wp	N	E
1	39 32.0100	2 33.8628
2	39 32.5302	2 34.1736
ALT	39 32.5641	2 34.2241
3	39 32.9208	2 33.7074
4	39 33.5082	2 33.1614
5	39 33.8790	2 33.9642
6	39 33.0456	2 34.1556

7	39 32.9958	2 34.5978
8	39 32.5764	2 35.3568

4.
CAP DE CALA FIGUERA

Wp	N	E
1	39 28.7970	2 31.3260
2	39 28.6284	2 31.2660
3	39 28.3500	2 31.2210
4	39 28.3092	2 31.3656
5	39 28.2756	2 31.3932
6	39 27.9132	2 31.3098
7	39 27.7608	2 31.1496
8	39 27.7122	2 31.1538
9	39 27.4956	2 31.2018
10	39 27.5694	2 30.9612
11	39 27.7788	2 30.4056
12	39 27.8340	2 30.2388
13	39 27.8004	2 30.1248
14	39 27.8814	2 30.1044
15	39 28.0122	2 30.0924
16	39 28.1514	2 30.0930
17	39 28.3110	2 30.1170
18	39 28.3794	2 30.2448
19	39 28.5942	2 30.5796
20	39 28.6878	2 30.8208
21	39 28.7250	2 30.8988
22	39 29.0070	2 31.1466

5.
CAMÍS DE CALVIA

Wp	N	E
A1	39 33.8106	2 27.6162
A2	39 34.2738	2 27.1830
A3	39 34.8636	2 27.5472

A4	39 34.9482	2 27.7812
B1	39 35.0346	2 27.7206
B2	39 34.8018	2 27.3636
C1	39 34.7640	2 28.1436
C2	39 35.0352	2 28.2084
C3	39 35.1588	2 28.4706
C4	39 35.0832	2 28.6164
D1	39 32.7606	2 31.0536
D2	39 33.0738	2 31.2126
D3	39 33.6240	2 31.9926
D4	39 34.1376	2 31.9566

6.
CALVIA TO SANTA PONÇA

Wp	N	E
1	39 33.9222	2 30.2214
2	39 33.8640	2 29.9550
3	39 32.6724	2 29.8488
4	39 32.1474	2 29.8716
5	39 31.4214	2 29.6028
6	39 31.0428	2 29.2668

7.
SANTA PONÇA: RACÓ DE SA FRAGATA

Wp	N	E
1	39 29.5140	2 28.8924
2	39 29.3820	2 29.0706
3	39 28.6536	2 28.9344
4	39 28.6278	2 29.1960
5	39 28.7700	2 28.9842

8.

PEGUERA: SA BRUTA

Wp	N	E
1	39 32.2446	2 26.7012
2	39 32.3688	2 26.7498
3	39 32.5866	2 26.4720
4	39 32.6520	2 26.4636
5	39 32.7636	2 26.5698
6	39 32.8536	2 26.6196
7	39 32.8380	2 26.6028
8	39 32.9502	2 26.5128
9	39 32.7204	2 26.4828
10	39 32.4960	2 26.1240
11	39 32.4216	2 26.3544
12	39 32.3688	2 26.6034
13	39 32.3346	2 26.6982

9.

PEGUERA: CAP ANDRITXOL (a) COURTING CLAUDIA

Wp	N	E
1	39 32.2218	2 26.6850
2	39 32.1972	2 26.5596
3	39 32.1294	2 26.3292
4	39 32.1036	2 26.2740
5	39 32.0886	2 26.0172
6	39 32.0244	2 25.9206
7	39 32.1300	2 25.6914
8	39 31.7400	2 25.4916
9	39 31.4862	2 25.3344
10	39 31.9350	2 25.5918
11	39 31.8936	2 25.8324
12	39 31.7556	2 25.8864
13	39 31.7484	2 25.9314
14	39 31.7574	2 26.1918
15	39 31.8678	2 26.1078
16	39 31.8636	2 26.2548
17	39 31.9974	2 26.2746

9.

PEGUERA: CAP ANDRITXOL (b) THE (ALMOST) UNCONTESTED ROUTE

Wp	N	E
1	39 31.8618	2 26.2518
2	39 31.8678	2 26.1078
3	39 31.7796	2 25.7310
4	39 31.7376	2 25.7094
5	39 31.6692	2 25.5768
6	39 31.7316	2 25.5228

10.

CAMP DE MAR TO ANDRATX OR PORT D'ANDRATX

Wp	N	E
1	39 32.4354	2 25.3962
2	39 32.2578	2 25.2966
3	39 32.3280	2 25.1436
4	39 32.4006	2 25.0860
5	39 32.4504	2 24.9456
6	39 32.3310	2 24.6912
7	39 32.2818	2 24.5484
8	39 32.2854	2 24.7158
9	39 32.2602	2 24.5742
10	39 32.2794	2 24.4842
11	39 32.2848	2 24.4386
12	39 32.2440	2 24.4122
13	39 32.2230	2 24.3570
14	39 32.2536	2 24.3276
15	39 32.3166	2 24.3000
16	39 32.3622	2 24.2838
17	39 32.4030	2 24.2118
18	39 32.4774	2 24.2256
19	39 32.5860	2 24.1266
20	39 32.7948	2 24.0318
21	39 33.0042	2 24.2490
22	39 33.0636	2 24.3300
23	39 33.2994	2 24.1404
24	39 33.5238	2 23.9826
25	39 33.6612	2 24.0810
26	39 33.7638	2 23.9160
27	39 34.3242	2 24.7830
28	39 34.5114	2 25.2042
29	39 32.6422	2 23.5597
30	39 32.7685	2 23.4454

11.

PORT D'ANRATX: CALA D'EGOS OR SANT ELM VIA ES TRES PICONS

Wp	N	E
1	39 33.1608	2 22.7274
2	39 33.1818	2 22.6986
3	39 33.2190	2 22.6656
4	39 33.2334	2 22.6392
5	39 33.2670	2 22.4574
6	39 33.2832	2 22.3788
7	39 33.3186	2 22.3218
8	39 33.8304	2 22.5306
9	39 34.0320	2 22.4646
10	39 34.2180	2 22.2102
11	39 33.8976	2 22.2876
12	39 33.6024	2 22.3272
13	39 33.3144	2 21.9774
14	39 33.2130	2 22.1076
15	39 33.2256	2 22.1904
16	39 33.2784	2 22.3032

12.

SANT ELM: SERRA D'EN PERXOTA & ES TRES PICONS

Wp	N	E
1	39 34.9770	2 20.9617
2	39 35.0892	2 21.1687
3	39 35.3982	2 21.3103
4	39 35.3592	2 21.4147
5	39 35.3364	2 21.8340
6	39 34.9158	2 22.1658
7	39 34.8240	2 22.6458
8	39 34.7898	2 22.6788
9	39 34.6716	2 22.7208
10	39 34.6116	2 22.5726
11	39 34.5288	2 22.3920
12	39 34.3260	2 22.1154
13	39 34.1994	2 22.0776
14	39 34.2996	2 22.0680
15	39 34.2522	2 21.8850
16	39 34.2048	2 21.6024
17	39 34.3896	2 21.3642
18	39 34.3908	2 21.2100

13.

S'ARRACO: PUIG D'EN FARINETA

Wp	N	E
1	39 34.7022	2 23.5242
2	39 34.6806	2 23.4306
3	39 34.9878	2 23.1474
4	39 35.1114	2 23.1162
5	39 35.0754	2 22.9218
6	39 35.1300	2 22.8924
7	39 35.1606	2 22.7730
8	39 35.2500	2 22.5234
9	39 35.2836	2 22.3242
10	39 35.2254	2 22.2318
11	39 35.1924	2 22.3224
12	39 35.0970	2 22.4262
13	39 35.0316	2 22.5414
14	39 34.9548	2 22.5876
15	39 34.8516	2 22.7376
16	39 34.8894	2 22.7976
17	39 35.1198	2 22.8528

14.
S'ARRACO: ES CASTELLESSETS

Wp	N	E
1	39 34.7004	2 23.5146
2	39 34.7874	2 23.5962
3	39 35.0124	2 23.6742
4	39 35.0370	2 23.7480
5	39 35.5608	2 23.5368
19-4	39 35.3430	2 22.9680
19-5	39 35.4414	2 22.7790
19-6	39 35.9016	2 23.0946
6	39 35.3850	2 23.1888
7	39 35.3868	2 23.1492
8	39 35.2458	2 23.2044

15.
ANDRATX: GARRAFA

Wp	N	E
1	39 34.3608	2 25.4898
2	39 34.2324	2 25.3584
3	39 34.0116	2 25.4052
4	39 33.6432	2 25.3920
5	39 33.5010	2 25.3584
6	39 33.4500	2 25.4256
7	39 33.5178	2 25.5192
8	39 33.5382	2 25.5672
9	39 33.5478	2 25.5654
10	39 33.5628	2 25.7028
11	39 33.5808	2 25.7694
12	39 33.6354	2 25.9200
13	39 33.6786	2 26.0190
14	39 33.7284	2 26.0604
15	39 33.9270	2 26.3130
16	39 34.0152	2 26.3244
17	39 34.3962	2 26.4180
18	39 34.7580	2 26.5776
19	39 34.8720	2 26.5506
20	39 34.4718	2 25.8462

16.
SANT ELM: CALA EN BASSET

Wp	N	E
1	39 34.9812	2 20.9640
2	39 35.0994	2 20.8902
3	39 35.0784	2 20.8386
4	39 35.1630	2 20.8284
5	39 35.2416	2 20.7996
6	39 35.3358	2 20.9466
7	39 35.4618	2 20.9412
8	39 35.5680	2 21.0438
9	39 35.6166	2 21.1416
10	39 35.7528	2 21.0504
11	39 35.6214	2 21.2064
12	39 35.6352	2 21.2760
13	39 35.7528	2 21.2772
14	39 35.6988	2 21.3192
15	39 35.5122	2 21.3372
16	39 35.4054	2 21.3252
17	39 35.1444	2 21.2502

17.
DRAGONERA: NA POPIA

Wp	N	E
1	39 35.2716	2 19.7022
2	39 35.2974	2 19.7058
3	39 35.2470	2 19.5528
4	39 35.2530	2 19.5222
5	39 35.3868	2 19.3854
6	39 35.3616	2 19.2972
7	39 35.0544	2 19.0212
8	39 35.1684	2 19.0356

18.
SA TRAPA FROM SANT ELM

Wp	N	E
1	39 34.9770	2 20.9616
2	39 35.0892	2 21.1686
3	39 35.3982	2 21.3102
4	39 35.3592	2 21.4146
5	39 35.3286	2 21.5808
6	39 35.3778	2 21.6564
7	39 35.4066	2 21.7386
8	39 35.4828	2 21.7656
9	39 35.6364	2 21.7506
10	39 35.7348	2 21.7998
11	39 35.8992	2 21.7836
12	39 35.9862	2 21.6336
13	39 35.9790	2 21.5004
14	39 35.9664	2 21.6600
15	39 35.8392	2 21.5274
16	39 35.5908	2 21.5058
17	39 35.5008	2 21.3372

19.
SA TRAPA FROM S'ARRACO

Wp	N	E
1	39 35.1558	2 23.0190
2	39 35.2632	2 23.1078
3	39 35.3796	2 23.1282
4	39 35.3430	2 22.9680
5	39 35.4414	2 22.7790
6	39 35.9016	2 23.0946
7	39 36.1038	2 23.0412
8	39 36.1164	2 23.1246
9	39 36.2514	2 22.9866
10	39 36.4500	2 22.9980
11	39 36.5101	2 22.8943
12	39 36.6055	2 22.6885
13	39 36.5911	2 22.1953
14	39 36.4117	2 22.2763
15	39 36.0204	2 21.8430

16	39 35. 9002	2 21.7728
17	39 35.3322	2 21.8370
18	39 34.8216	2 22.6344

20.
SA TRAPA FROM ANDRATX

Wp	N	E
1	39 34.6482	2 25.2744
2	39 34.6536	2 24.8892
3	39 35.1372	2 24.9486
4	39 35.5272	2 25.1526
5	39 36.1044	2 25.0512
6	39 36.2868	2 24.5454
7	39 36.4188	2 24.0888
8	39 36.2922	2 23.8530
9	39 36.4470	2 23.0028
10	39 36.5100	2 22.8942
11	39 36.6414	2 22.7232
12	39 36.6054	2 22.6884
13	39 36.5910	2 22.1952
14	39 36.6108	2 22.1346
15	39 36.4116	2 22.2762
16	39 36.0240	2 21.8406

21.
ESTELLENCS: S'ESCLOP

Wp	N	E
1	39 38.7852	2 27.7242
2	39 38.6952	2 27.9210
3	39 38.6076	2 28.0806
4	39 38.4906	2 28.1286
5	39 38.4048	2 28.0434
6	39 38.3448	2 28.0128
7	39 38.2854	2 27.9168
8	39 38.2470	2 27.8430
9	39 38.1492	2 27.8214
10	39 38.1084	2 27.7698
11	39 38.0118	2 27.5766
12	39 37.9446	2 27.5520
13	39 37.9362	2 27.4278
14	39 37.9224	2 27.3708
15	39 37.7916	2 27.2100
16	39 37.7670	2 27.0120
17	39 37.8030	2 26.9298
18	39 37.8018	2 26.8710
19	39 37.7574	2 26.7066
20	39 37.6722	2 26.6802
21	39 37.6056	2 26.6724
22	39 37.6068	2 26.7480
23	39 37.5234	2 26.7708
24	39 37.4790	2 26.7696
25	39 37.5138	2 26.6946

22.
(a) GALATZÓ FROM THE NORTH (ESTELLENCS)

Wp	N	E
A1	39 38.7636	2 27.7260
A2	39 38.6994	2 27.9204
A3	39 38.6184	2 28.0830
A4	39 38.4942	2 28.1226
A5	39 38.5554	2 28.3746
A6	39 38.3478	2 29.1030
A7	39 38.2296	2 29.1372
A8	39 38.0370	2 29.2008
A9	39 38.2698	2 29.4072
A10	39 38.8248	2 28.2876

22.
(b) GALATZÓ FROM THE SOUTH (PUIGPUNYENT)

Wp	N	E
B1	39 37.2132	2 31.5144
B2	39 37.1826	2 30.2034
B3	39 37.5942	2 29.9742
B4	39 37.6056	2 29.7966
B5	39 37.8012	2 29.6496
B6	39 37.9362	2 29.6508
B7	39 38.1222	2 29.6262
B8	39 38.1210	2 29.5344
B9	39 38.1390	2 29.3688

23.
THE NORTHERN PORTS (a) ESTELLENCS

Wp	N	E
A1	39 39.1956	2 28.8696
A2	39 39.0894	2 28.6734
A3	39 39.4896	2 28.2510
A4	39 39.4914	2 28.2828
A5	39 39.4626	2 28.4610
A6	39 39.3960	2 28.5354
A7	39 39.3582	2 28.6626
A8	39 39.3942	2 28.8060
A9	39 39.3630	2 28.7790

23.
THE NORTHERN PORTS (b) SA PEDRA DE S'ASE

Wp	N	E
B1	39 40.9692	2 30.0132
B2	39 40.6434	2 29.7498
B3	39 40.7292	2 29.6652

23.
THE NORTHERN PORTS (c) BANYALBUFAR

Wp	N	E
C1	39 41.2932	2 30.9630
C2	39 41.3160	2 30.9738
C3	39 41.4396	2 31.0242
C4	39 41.4300	2 30.9708
C5	39 41.4846	2 30.8760
C6	39 41.2386	2 30.8214

24.
GR221: BANYALBUFAR TO ESTELLENCS

Wp	N	E
1	39 41.1852	2 30.7548
2	39 41.1948	2 30.6720
3	39 41.1474	2 30.6324
4	39 41.0292	2 30.4644
5	39 40.9698	2 30.3696
6	39 40.9428	2 30.2910
7	39 40.8396	2 30.1092
8	39 40.7844	2 30.0306
9	39 40.7370	2 30.0168
10	39 40.5348	2 29.9346
11	39 40.2978	2 29.9748
12	39 40.2258	2 29.9742
13	39 40.2264	2 29.5998
14	39 39.9018	2 29.3430
15	39 39.7752	2 29.2716
16	39 39.5352	2 29.0466
17	39 39.5190	2 29.0424
18	39 39.4392	2 29.0874
19	39 39.3306	2 29.1150
20	39 39.3138	2 29.0502

25.
ESPORLES TO BANYALBUFAR VIA PORT D'ES CANONGE: CAMÍ DE PESCADORS & SA VOLTA DES GENERAL

Wp	N	E
1	39 40.1268	2 34.6470
2	39 40.3164	2 34.7196
3	39 40.5678	2 34.6476
4	39 40.4766	2 34.2282
5	39 40.6206	2 33.9774
6	39 40.6884	2 33.9858
7	39 40.7766	2 33.8874
8	39 40.7814	2 33.7920
9	39 41.1486	2 33.5664
10	39 41.1306	2 33.3876
11	39 41.2038	2 33.5574
12	39 41.3286	2 33.4176
13	39 41.4378	2 33.3762
14	39 41.5026	2 33.2370
15	39 41.9694	2 33.2952
16	39 41.9196	2 33.0096
17	39 41.8380	2 32.5404
18	39 41.8098	2 32.4540
19	39 41.9382	2 31.9530
20	39 41.7114	2 31.4682
21	39 41.4564	2 31.1724
22	39 41.4366	2 31.1088
23	39 41.4318	2 31.0248
24	39 41.2890	2 30.9558

26.
BANYALBUFAR TO ESPORLES: CAMÍ DES CORREU

Wp	N	E
1	39 41.2356	2 30.8298
2	39 41.0418	2 31.2978
3	39 41.0298	2 31.3734
4	39 40.9182	2 31.7820
5	39 40.8318	2 31.9476
6	39 40.7826	2 32.6100
7	39 40.8144	2 32.7084
8	39 40.6056	2 33.1206
9	39 40.4106	2 33.2862
10	39 40.3542	2 33.6348
11	39 40.1316	2 34.0746
12	39 40.1154	2 34.2702

27.
ESPORLES: SA FITA DEL RAM

Wp	N	E
1	39 39.9474	2 34.7640
2	39 39.7512	2 34.7478
3	39 39.6534	2 34.7976
4	39 39.5496	2 34.7796
5	39 39.5460	2 34.5546
6	39 39.5856	2 34.4808
7	39 39.4302	2 34.4172
8	39 39.4548	2 34.3392
9	39 39.5262	2 34.2048
10	39 39.7206	2 34.0068
11	39 39.7764	2 34.0350
12	39 39.6978	2 33.9492
13	39 39.6354	2 33.7422
14	39 39.5568	2 33.6066
15	39 39.5052	2 33.6048
16	39 39.4266	2 33.4890
17	39 39.3936	2 33.3516
18	39 39.4290	2 33.2790
19	39 39.3216	2 33.0234
20	39 39.2118	2 33.0300
21	39 39.1530	2 33.0774
22	39 38.9880	2 33.1116

28.
PUIGPUNYENT: ES PUNTALS DE SON FORTESA

Wp	N	E
1	39 37.8102	2 31.5786
2	39 38.1492	2 31.0548
3	39 38.1312	2 30.9726
SC1	39 38.1258	2 30.7104
SC2	39 38.1438	2 30.6636
4	39 38.3490	2 30.6450
5	39 38.5074	2 30.5604
6	39 38.5890	2 30.5022
7	39 38.6796	2 30.5682
8	39 38.8860	2 30.6294
9	39 38.8602	2 30.4260
10	39 38.9178	2 30.3936
11	39 39.2244	2 30.3108
12	39 39.2718	2 30.3504
13	39 39.2634	2 30.3714
14	39 39.2790	2 30.4410
15	39 39.2754	2 30.4434
16	39 38.8632	2 31.0044
17	39 39.0276	2 31.2096
18	39 38.6328	2 31.9326
19	39 38.3670	2 31.7958

29.
PUIGPUNYENT TO CALVIÁ

Wp	N	E
1	unreliable	record
2	39 36.8514	2 31.1790
3	39 36.6762	2 30.9846
4	39 36.5142	2 30.7758
5	39 36.2328	2 30.8244
6	39 35.6328	2 30.7608
7	39 35.2682	2 30.7704
8	39 35.2158	2 30.7182
9	39 34.9896	2 30.7200
10	39 34.7934	2 30.5790
11	39 34.5750	2 30.4476
12	39 33.9618	2 30.4056

30.
GALILEA: PUIG DE NA BAUÇANA

Wp	N	E
1	39 36.5202	2 30.7758
2	39 36.4206	2 30.7998
3	39 36.3252	2 30.7500
4	39 36.2304	2 30.8106
5	39 36.1746	2 30.8136
6	39 36.3750	2 30.8850
7	39 36.2232	2 30.8970
8	39 36.1800	2 31.1220
9	39 36.2646	2 31.1040

GLOSSARY

This glossary contains Spanish and Catalán words found in the text (shown in *italics*) plus other local words that you may encounter.

Please note that the spelling of place names and other local words on signs and maps can vary according to local conventions.

SPANISH	CATALÁN	
a		
agua, con/sin gas		water, fizzy/still
aljibe	*aljub*	ancient cistern/reservoir
alto	*dalt*	high, upper
área recreativa		picnic spot, usually with barbecues, toilets, water
atalaya	*atalaya*	ancient watch-tower
avenida	*avinguda*	avenue
ayuntamiento	*ayuntament*	town hall
b		
bajo	*baix*	low
bajo	*avall*	lower
barranco	*barranc*	gorge, ravine
botadores		stone steps in country walls
c		
cala		creek, small bay, sometimes just a tiny coastal indentation
calle	*carrer*	street
camino	*camí*	road, path or way
camino real	*camí real*	royal road, once a major donkey trail
campo		countryside, field
	ca, can, c'an	house of
canaleta	*siquia*	man-made water channel, including anything from a concrete canal to delicately arched aqueducts
calle	*carrer*	street
carritx	*carritx*	pampas-like grass
casa	*can/ca*	house of (as *chez* in French)
casa de nieve	*casa neu*	snow pit/ice house
caseta		hut, cabin, small house
cingles		cliffs, crags; most often used to describe the sort of short,abrupt cliffs that typically define the rounded summits of many Catalán and Mallorcan mountains
ciudad	*ciutat*	city
coll	*collada*	saddle, neck or pass
correos		post office
costa		coast
cueva	*cova*	cave
e		
embalse		reservoir
ermita		hermitage, small church, shrine
f		
faro		lighthouse
fiesta		festival, public holiday
finca	*lluc*	farm
forn de calc	*horno de calç*	lime kiln
fuente	*font*	spring, well
h		
hostal		hostel, simple accommodation

l

lavadero		public laundry area
llano	**pla**	plain, flat land

m

medio	**mig**	middle
mercado	**mercat**	market
mirador		viewing point, sometimes with man-made facilities, more often a natural place with a good view
morro		snout or muzzle, a rounded summit

p

parada		bus stop
parque natural	**parc natural**	natural park
particular		private
paseo	**passeig**	walkway
peatones		pedestrians
peña	**penya/penyal**	rock or boulder, used for a knoll or pinnacle on a ridge
pico	**puig**	translates as 'hill' or 'height', though more often a peak or mountain
pista		dirt road
pista forestal		forest road
planicie	**pla**	plain
plato combinado		lit. combined plate, a restaurant dish including (usually) meat or fish, vegetables or salad, and potatoes
playa	**platja**	beach
plaza	**plaça**	town square
pozo	**pou**	well
privado		private
prohibido el paso		no entry
puerto	**port**	port, mountain pass

r

refugio		mountain refuge, some offering basic overnight accommodation
	rota	mountain smallholding with cabin

s

santo/a	**san/sant**	saint
santuario	**santuari**	monastery, hermitage
sendero	**senda**	footpath, trail
sierra	**serra**	mountain range
sitja (pl. sitjes)	**sitja**	charcoal burning area or circle
su	**son, sa, ses**	his, her, their

t

tipico		typical, locals' café/bar
toro bravo		wild bull
torre		tower, often a coastal watchtower built to warn of approaching pirates, or a Moorish lookout tower
torrente	**torrent**	stream

u

urbanización	**urbanració**	housing development

v

viejo	**vell**	old

A USEFUL INFORMATION

Please note:
Telephone numbers are shown in red, and fax numbers in blue, and we show the entire number you need to dial from outside Spain. From within Spain (including its islands), omit the 00 34. Websites and email addresses are shown in green.

GETTING A BED

www.mallorca.com/english/

If you want to arrange your own accommodation and want to stay somewhere off the usual tourism run, then try:

Alternative Tourism

00 34 971 768040   00 34 971 768248
rusticrent@baleares.com
www.rusticrent.com

Agrotourism, Rural Hotels & Fincas

00 34 971 717122   00 34 971 717977
info@davimar.com
www.mallorcaonline.com

S'Hostal Esporles 00 34 971 610202   00 34 971 611763
Plaça d'Espanya
07190 Esporles   hostalesporles@futurnet.es

- is exquisite in every respect: the restoration, the decoration, the general good taste, the welcome, the peacefulness, the food, and for some appetites the portions, too. Pricey (€40-50 per head, breakfast included), but highly recommended.

GETTING ABOUT

www.mallorca.com/english/

Boats

www.barcosazules.com

Buses

www.autocaresmallorca.com

Ferries

www.trasmediterranea.es

MISCELLANEOUS

Emergencies (equivalent to the UK's 999 service) Tel. 112

Tourist Information Office
Plaça de la Reina, 2
Palma 07012   00 34 971 712216   0043 971 720251
Balearic Islands   turisme@a-palma.es
SPAIN

This is the island's main office. Most resorts have their own offices but these may only be open during the main tourist season of approximately Easter to October.

Palma Tourist Information (Head Office)
Plaça d'Espanya
Edificio Parc de ses Estacions
07002 Palma   00 34 971 715741
SPAIN   palmainfo@a-palma.es

Airport Information Office
Palma Airport
07000 Palma   00 34 971 789556
SPAIN

Oficina Española de Turísmo
22-23 Manchester Square
London W1M 5AP   www.tourspain.es

General Information
www.caib.es
www.ensaimadablau.com
www.balearnet.com
www.mallorca.com/english/
www.mallorcaservice.com
www.visitbalears.com
www.a2zmallorca.com

Consell de Mallorca (the island's government)

www.conselldemallorca.net

Meteorology   www.inm.es/cmt/palm

Tourist Guides
www.apitmallorca.com

FOOD AND DRINK

For a cheap bed and good, authentic Italian food, try the **Trattoria Italia** in **Peguera**. It's really very Italian and virtually every order, from a full scale meal to a simple coffee, is followed by a free glass of grappa.

For excellent food and a very pleasant atmosphere, try the **Rancho Romana** on the C719 just east of the **Peguera/Romana** turn-off. There's a walk to be done in the estates behind the **Rancho Romana**, but access is limited and only permitted in a guided group. If interested, inquire in the **Peguera Tourist Information Office**. The guided walk is free.

For an authentic Mallorcan drinking experience (zinc bar, cheerfully bibulous old men, and stacks of personal playing cards), head for **Bar C'as Pobil** in **Andratx** central *plaza* and the **Café Deportiu** on the main drag in **Esporles**.

S'Hostal Esporles - is exquisite in every respect and offers accommodation and good food. For contact details see under **Getting A Bed** earlier in this appendix.

In **Esporles**, **Es Brollador** is an attractive little restaurant serving *platos combinados* during the day and a slightly more sophisticated a la carte menu in the evening.

Montimar in **Estellencs** is an excellent restaurant drawing in locals as well as tourists.

B BIBLIOGRAPHY

Please note that some of these titles may be difficult to obtain or out of print, but most can be purchased second hand or new on
www.amazon.co.uk

GENERAL BOOKS ABOUT MALLORCA IN ENGLISH

Wild Olives: Life in Mallorca by William Graves (Pimlico) What Dad did after all that. £8.99 **ISBN 0-712601-16-3**

Snowball Oranges: A Winter's Take on a Spanish Isle Peter Kerr (Lyons Press) Peter Mayle, Chris Stewart et al **ISBN 1-585748-66-8**

A Winter In Majorca George Sand (various editions). Bitter about Mallorcans £5.99. **ISBN 1-899865-37-3**

Birds of the Balearic Islands Muddeman, Hearl & Busby (A&C Black) £27.00 **ISBN 0-713665-33-5**

Field Guide to Wild Flowers of Southern Europe Paul Davies and Bob Gibbons (Crowood Press) £10.99 **ISBN 1-852236-59-0**

LOCALLY PUBLISHED BOOKS IN ENGLISH

Folk Tales of Mallorca Mn. Alcover (Moll) **ISBN 8-427308-22-1**

Wild Orchids of Mallorca Nicole T. Beniston & William S. Beniston (Moll) £7.80 **ISBN 8-427308-24-8**

Plants of the Balearic Islands Anthony Bonner (Moll) **ISBN 8-427304-23-4**

Bread & Oil (Prospect) £12.36 **ISBN 0-299179-90-7** *and* **A Home in Majorca** Tomá Graves (Foradada)

Birds of the Balearic Islands Joan Mayol (Moll)

Discovering the Art of Mallorcan Cooking Toby Molenar (Moll)

Majorca The Island of Calm Santiago Rusiñ

WALKING GUIDES IN ENGLISH

Walk! Mallorca (North & Mountains) Charles Davis (Discovery Walking Guides Ltd) £11.99 **ISBN 1-899554-92-0**
Highly recommended companion volume to this publication.

Walking in Mallorca June Parker (Cicerone) £14.99
ISBN 1-8952842-50-4
All ramblers in Mallorca owe a huge debt to June Parker, who first described many routes even the locals hadn't published. However, June sadly died in 1998 and there has been no comprehensive updating of the book. Given the changes that have taken place on the island, this book is falling increasingly out of date.

Holiday Walks in Mallorca Graham Beech (Sigma) £9.95
ISBN 1-850587-38-8

Landscapes of Mallorca Valerie Crespí-Green (Sunflower) £9.99
ISBN 1-856912-04-3

Mallorca Rolf Goetz (Rother) £7.99 **ISBN 3-763348-05-0**

WALKING GUIDES IN CATALÁN

Lluis Vallcanares has published several guides, including three volumes of itineraries suitable for children **Descobrim Tramuntana** (Gorg Blau) (Vol. 1. 6-8 years old, Vol. 2. 8-10 years old, Vol. 3. 10-12 years old) and two volumes of **20 Itineraris Alternatius** (Gorg Blau).

MAPS FOR WALKERS

Mallorca North & Mountains Tour & Trail Super-Durable Map 1:40,000 scale (Discovery Walking Guides Ltd) £7.99 **ISBN 1-899554-93-9**
Companion map to **Walk! Mallorca (North & Mountains)**.

Two Spanish organisations publish the closest equivalents to traditional Ordnance Survey style maps. They are:-

Centro Nacional de Información Geográfica
Oficina Central, Monte Esquinza, 41
28010 Madrid
SPAIN   00 34 91 5979453   00 34 91 5532913
www.cnig.es
consulta@cnig.es.

Servicio Geográfico del Ejército
Dario Gazapo, 8
28024 Madrid
SPAIN   00 34 91 7115043   00 34 91 7115033

AERIAL PHOTOGRAPHS
This excellent book of aerial photographs of the Mallorcan coastline is available (in Spain) in a large size and mini version.

Aeroguía del Litoral de Mallorca (mini) (Geoplaneta) €11.42
ISBN 0-80256-69-4
El Litoral de Mallorca (Geoplaneta) €29 **ISBN 8-408039-39-3**

C CYCLE ROUTES

Roads suitable for cycling:

A There are miles of cycling paths between **Bendinat** and **Santa Ponça**, far too many to itemize.

B the **Cala Fornells** / **Cap de Cala Figuera** road from **Magaluf**

C PMV-1016 **Establiments** to **Calvià**

D PMV-1031 **Andratx** to **Capdellá**

E PMV-1032 **Capdella** to **Puigpunyent**

F PMV-1041&1042 **Puigpunyent** to **Establiments**

G PMV-1043 **Palma de Mallorca** to the PMV-1016 (see 3 above)

H PMV-1101 **Puigpunyent** to **Esporles**

I the **Camí de Son Pillo** between **Calvià** & the PMV-1014

J the **Camí de Molí Nou** between **Camí de Son Pillo** & **Capdella**

K PM102 **Port Andratx** to **Camp de Mar**

L PM103 **Andratx** to **Sant Elm**

M the unnumbered road from the C710 down to **Port d'es Canonge** (see Walk 25)

N the **Es Verger** road from **Esporles**, climbing via **Sobremunt** and descending to the PMV1041 (see 6 above)

O PM104 **Esporles** to **Establiments**

Walking itineraries in this book suitable for mountain bikes:

1   Serra de Son Camps: Pujol des Gat

2   Na Burguesa: Mirador de n'Alzamora

3   Na Burguesa: Puig Gros de Bendinat

4   Cap de Cala Figuera (following the road to **Portals Vells**)

Calvià *ayuntamiento* pay various landowners to keep the **Romana** route from **Peguera** to **Calvià** open, but since access is limited and only permitted to organized groups, it is not an appropriate itinerary for a book like this. If interested in joining one of the free guided walks, enquire in **Peguera Tourist Office**.

The **Son Fortuny** estate behind **Camp de Mar** has posted notices explicitly prohibiting walkers. Nothing was said about skateboarding, but I didn't feel like pushing my luck.

The **S'Atalaya** walk above **Cala des Llamp** is still open, *prohibido el paso* signs notwithstanding, but a couple of new villas overlooking **Camp de Mar** suggest this may not be the case for long. If you want to try it, drive up from **Port d'Andratx** to the edge of the **Urbanizació Gran Folies** (there's a mapboard of the itinerary en route) and keep turning left till you come to the end of the road at locked gates. A version of this walk appears in Graham Beech's Holiday Walks In Mallorca.

The **Puig d'es Cornadors** walk, signposted at the start of the **Capdella** road next to **Andratx** *ayuntamiento* is still accessible, but again, boys with bags of cement and piles of breezeblocks are up there messing about, so I don't know what the future holds.

The **Puig de Sa Na Vidala** walk, illustrated in the flimsy leaflet from **Andratx** *ayuntamiento*, was simply one too many for the area. It can be reached via the start of Walk 20.

The **GR221** between **Coll de sa Gramola** and **Estellencs** involves 2 kilometres on the road. A new route is being planned, but no more than that at present.

The **Camí Vell** from **Estellencs** to **Puigpunyent** should be a good way of beginning a tour of the **Estellencs Son Fortuny** estate. Unfortunately, despite being published elsewhere, it doesn't exist! Or at least the **Estellencs** end currently involves crossing the private **Son Fortuny** estate. The gates are open, but…

The classic corniche path above **Banyalbufar**, the **Camí de Planí y es Rafal**, crosses the **Es Rafal** estate, starting on the same path as Walk 24, and I felt two itineraries on a disputed right of way was one too many. Court case pending…

The route of the **GR221** from **Esporles** to **Valldemossa** is currently being negotiated. I don't know where precisely it will go, but I understand it is unlikely to follow the route described by June Parker in Walking In Mallorca.

The climb up **Planicia** via **Son Vic** crosses several farms and I was unable to ascertain whether all the landowners were still amenable to this, though the presence of a new ladder stile and the absence of private-property notices suggest the owner of **Son Vic** has no objections to ramblers crossing his land.

Something to look forward to in the next edition!

Several routes were excluded as they required asking permission each time they were used. All other lacunae are the result of ignorance. Any enlightening suggestions are more than welcome.

WALK! GUIDEBOOKS
(backed by our 'no compromise' research policy)

Spending a lot of our time amongst dramatic landscapes, we appreciate the value of an accurately researched and well written walk description. Abroad, in a foreign land, is no place to find yourself lost and in danger. Knowing this, we operate a 'no compromise' policy for all DWG walking routes. Every route is walked - repeatedly if necessary - to make sure that we have an accurate walk description. Then we try to write a detailed walk description in an inspirational tone so that you know how we felt on that route. We've slogged up that impossible looking ascent, marvelled at those panoramas, found paths through apparently pathless wilderness, have gratefully arrived at our destination. It's not always fun, but it has always been an adventure. Our GPS ground survey system means that we know exactly where we've been, except when there is poor GPS reception and we tell you this.

This 'no compromise 'policy is much appreciated by users of DWG walking guides, to which our post bag testifies. This means that, with a DWG guidebook, you can confidently embark on the adventures it contains, knowing that every route is researched to the highest standard.

We still marvel at every "Your guide made my holiday"letter we receive, just as we did at the first one we ever received. Bringing adventure and enjoyment to people is very pleasing, and we are very good listeners to what our readers would like to appear in a walk description.

In Walk! Mallorca (West) you'll find:-

- walking route summary including Effort, Time, Distance, Ascents/Descents, and Refreshments
- frequent timings so that you can judge your progress against Charles Davis
- fully detailed, and inspirational, walk description
- detailed map for every walking route
- GPS Waypoints (grid references) for key points on the route
- full GPS Waypoint lists for all walking routes
- national and regional Locator Maps
- lots of useful background information

We haven't done all this just because Walk! Mallorca (West) is special, which it certainly is; this is our normal 'no compromise'approach to giving you everything you need in a walking guide book. Now, go out there and enjoy it, safe in the knowledge that Charles has been there before, and that we have a full GPS track and waypoint record of where he has been. Generally our routes are straightforward, so long as you follow the walk descriptions. All that's necessary is for you to be there, marvelling at the beautiful landscapes, the amazing flora and fauna, and making masses of new discoveries.

If you are a GPS/PC user you may be interested to know that all the GPS Tracks and Waypoints for Walk! Mallorca (West) are available, for downloading direct to your GPS, on our Personal Navigator Files CD along with hundreds more walking routes from our Walk! guidebooks.

David & Ros Brawn
Directors of Discovery Walking Guides Ltd.

HOW TO GET HOLD OF OUR PUBLICATIONS

See the list of UK stockists on the back page or order direct from us by mail order, using the form below, or write to us at the address below.

If you are ordering direct from us, please:
- complete your details in BLOCK CAPITALS
- write the full title(s) of the publications you require
- enclose your payment (please note that post & packing is free)
- make your cheque payable to:

Discovery Walking Guides Ltd.
and post to:
Discovery Walking Guides Ltd.
10 Tennyson Close
Northampton NN5 7HJ

TITLE(S) ORDERED	ITEM COST

I enclose my cheque for this **TOTAL**
(free post & packing)

YOUR NAME

ADDRESS

POST CODE

*TEL N°

**email   @

* for order enquiries only   ** for enewsletters and updates

DISCOVERY WALKING GUIDES LTD.TITLES LIST

GPS

GPS The Easy Way
Manual **£4.99**
Personal Navigator Files - CD
(Oziexplorer format) **Version 2.01 £7.99**

SPANISH MAINLAND

Sierra de Aracena - a Walk! Guidebook
Guidebook **£11.99**
Sierra de Aracena
Tour & Trail Map **£2.99**
34 Alpujarras Walks
Guidebook **£9.99**
Alpujarras Super-Durable
Tour & Trail Map **£7.99**

CANARY ISLANDS

Walk! Lanzarote
Guidebook **£11.99**
Lanzarote Super-Durable
Tour & Trail Map **£7.99**
Lanzarote   Indestructible Map **£4.99**
Lanzarote   Plant&Flower Guide **£2**

Walk! La Gomera (2nd edition)
Guidebook **£11.99**
La Gomera Super-Durable
Tour &Trail Map **£7.99**
Drive! La Gomera
Touring Map **£2.50**
La Gomera   Plant&Flower Guide **£2**

35 Tenerife Walks
Guidebook **£9.99**
Walk! Tenerife South
Guidebook **£5.99**
Tenerife Super-Durable
Walkers' Maps **£4.99**
Tenerife Paper Edition
Walkers' Maps **£2.99**
Tenerife   Indestructible Map **£4.99**

Drive! Tenerife Touring Map **£2.50**

Tenerife   Plant&Flower Guide **£2**

Gran Canaria Mountains
Tour & Trail Map **£5**
Gran Canaria Plant&Flower Guide **£2**

Walk! La Palma
Guidebook **£11.99**
La Palma Super-Durable
Tour & Trail Map **£7.99**

BALEARIC ISLANDS

Walk! Mallorca (North & Mountains)
Guidebook **£11.99**
Mallorca North & Mountains Super-Durable
Tour & Trail Map **£7.99**
Walk! Mallorca West
Guidebook **£11.99**

Walk! Menorca
Guidebook **£11.99**
Menorca Super-Durable
Tour & Trail Map **£7.99**

ANDORRA

Walk! Andorra
Guidebook **£11.99**

PORTUGAL, INCLUDING MADEIRA

Madeira Super-Durable
Tour & Trail Map **£7.99**
35 Madeira Walks
Guidebook **£9.99**

Algarve - Loule
Walking Guide **£5**
Algarve - Silves
Walking Guide **£5**

MALTA & GOZO

Malta & Gozo Walking Guides **£5**

DWG Ltd.
10 Tennyson Close
Northampton NN5 7HJ
www.walking.demon.co.uk
www.dwgwalking.co.uk

The Map Shop
Upton Upon Severn
Tel: 01684 593146
themapshop@btinternet.com
www.themapshop.co.uk

Stanfords Bookshops
Tel: 020 7759 7137
sales@stanfords.co.uk
www.stanfords.co.uk

- or ask in bookshops